RULES

of the

HUNT

RULES

of the

HUNT

Real-World Advice for Entrepreneurial and Business Success

MICHAEL DALTON JOHNSON

New York   Chicago   San Francisco   Lisbon   London   Madrid   Mexico City
Milan   New Delhi   San Juan   Seoul   Singapore   Sydney   Toronto

1 2 3 4 5 6 7 8 9 10   DOC/DOC   1 9 8 7 6 5 4 3 2

ISBN   978-0-07-179138-0
MHID   0-07-179138-8

e-ISBN   978-0-07-179139-7
e-MHID 0-07-179139-6

Library of Congress Cataloging-in-Publication Data
Johnson, Michael Dalton.
   Rules of the hunt : outfox the competition for entrepreneurial and business success / by Michael Dalton Johnson.
      p. cm.
   ISBN 978-0-07-179138-0 (alk. paper)—ISBN 0-07-179138-8 (alk. paper)
   1. New business enterprises—Management. 2. Entrepreneurship. 3. Success in business. I. Title.
   HD62.5.J636 2012
   658.1'1—dc23   2011044680

McGraw-Hill books are available at special quantity discounts to use as premiums and sales promotions or for use in corporate training programs. To contact a representative, please e-mail us at bulksales@mcgraw-hill.com.

This book is printed on acid-free paper.

For Kathryn

Contents

Covers the many unexpected challenges and opportunities entrepreneurs encounter that are never part of a formal business education.

Rules for developing leadership, which is an essential element of entrepreneurial success. Subtle, yet profoundly effective ways to create loyalty, inspire trust, and motivate others.

Advice on forming strong and long-lasting business bonds with customers, employees, suppliers, and investors that are money in the bank.

Winning a One-Horse Race

BY JEFFREY GITOMER

WHEN I WAS a sophomore in college, my friend and I bought a standard bred racehorse. It was a claiming race, and we had the money, so we decided to take a risk and have some fun.

It was my first real business venture. The horse won its second race, and I got to go down to the winner's circle for a photo op. What a feeling. What a rush. What a great business venture.

Fast-forward six months, and I learned another lesson: Horses eat lots of hay. And if the costs of food, care, and stable rental are greater than your winnings, you're in a losing situation.

I wasn't just a horse owner, I was in the business of making money. Making hay to buy hay.

Whether you are an entrepreneur, sales professional, or business owner, you are in the race of your life — against yourself. Winning or losing that race is in your hands. Your success will depend on what actions you take every day, the decisions you make, the experiences you have, and, most importantly, the lessons you learn from each.

Every one of you has a half-dozen stories attached to a sales success or a sales failure that has affected your success, your fortune, and your life. Stories form the core of emotional engagement, emotional attachment, and emotional connection when they are told with passion.

In *Rules of the Hunt*, Michael Dalton Johnson gives you real-world business and life advice to help you win your race. He tells memorable business stories and presents lessons about integrity, about money, about reality, about failure, and about life. These lessons are authentic and insightful, and they will have an impact on your thinking, your career, your success, and your personal fulfillment.

Michael's stories are real, relatable, and actionable. Stories that will help you find your brass ring, pot of gold at the end of the rainbow, golden ticket, or winning lottery ticket, otherwise known as *business success*.

The lessons that are imparted in these modern-day stories will help you in the same way they helped Michael. Each chapter, each set of stories, is to be taken one at a time so that you can integrate his lessons into your knowledge.

I have reached millions through my best-selling books and internationally syndicated sales and business growth column. I conduct 100 live conferences and seminars each year. I am proud to have earned the title of America's number one sales trainer.

What many people often don't consider when they read my books or attend my seminars is that I am first and foremost an entrepreneur. And I come from a family of entrepreneurs.

I've been in business for myself for over four decades. I have built a team of people who share my entrepreneurial vision and have helped me create and deliver a wide range of personal development products and services to business and sales professionals worldwide.

Along the journey there were opportunities to be seized and obstacles to be overcome. Each one has given me a valuable business and life lesson. Entrepreneurial success is both earned and learned.

That may be what attracted you to this book.

As a writer and speaker over the past 20 years, I have met and shaken hands with tens of thousands of people. I have learned that the most common trait shared by those I've reached is their desire to gain the knowledge they need to succeed.

While everyone wants to succeed in the world, the smart ones know that success comes with learning and experience. I have raised a few eyebrows by zealously teaching that passion and emotions are essential to achieving business and personal objectives.

I believe that success comes from both the head and the heart.

This book has a lion's share of emotion. It is an entertaining and informative collection of the author's experiences and observations on achieving entrepreneurial goals.

Michael shares a lifetime of learning, a lifetime of teaching, and a lifetime of earning. He is offering these stories to you so that you might learn his hard-earned lessons in advance, saving you time, saving you money, saving your health and sanity, and in some cases, saving your rear end.

These lessons are not just about business and life; they also serve as preventive medicine. Every day of your business life you will encounter the same roadblocks and pitfalls that Michael has already experienced and conquered.

Rules of the Hunt captures the essence of everyday real-world business — the things that actually happen. Because of this, *Rules of the Hunt* offers lessons that every reader will relate to and profit from. The central message of this book is that, in the end, reaching success is about you. Read it, enjoy it, understand it, and use it to help you win your race.

Jeffrey Gitomer

Jeffrey Gitomer is a renowned sales trainer and motivational speaker. He is the author of the bestselling The Sales Bible, The Little Red Book of Selling, The Little Red Book of Sales, The Little Green Book of Getting Your Way, *and many other popular business books. His website is www.gitomer.com.*

Acknowledgments

YOU'LL FIND NO flattery here. This is sincere praise of friends and family who, through their encouragement and intelligent advice, have helped and inspired me in the creation of this book.

Colette Lynch has been a true miracle worker who came to the project at precisely the right time. Without her emcouragement, guidance, and organizational abilities, this book would not exist.

A special thanks to Jane Palmieri at McGraw-Hill for her editorial wisdom and patience.

Thanks to Elliot Bornin, one of the most interesting people I've ever met and an editorial advisor of enormous talent.

Thanks are also due my agent and trusted confidant, John Willig, whose buoyant spirit and priceless publishing advice will always be remembered with gratitude.

I acknowledge and thank my friend Cheryl Close for her editorial help, and I express my gratitude to Lynda Goodman for kick-starting the project and to my longtime colleague Tina LoSasso for her marketing witchcraft.

Finally, I want to thank my family for their understanding and support, not only during the writing of this book, but also through my entire business career. I love you all.

Disclaimer

NOTHING IN THIS book should be considered prescriptive.

This book is designed to provide information and motivation to readers. It is sold with the understanding that neither the publisher nor the author are engaged in rendering any type of psychological, legal, or other kind of professional advice.

The content of each chapter is the sole expression and opinion of the author and not necessarily that of the publisher. No warranties or guarantees are expressed or implied by the publisher's or author's choice to include any of the content in this book.

Neither the publisher nor the author shall be liable for any physical, psychological, emotional, financial, or commercial damages, including, but not limited to, special, incidental, consequential or other damages. Our views and rights are the same: You are responsible for your own choices, actions, and results.

Let's Cut to the Chase

THIS BOOK WON'T make you rich or successful. That's your job.

If you are intelligent and ambitious, you have a good chance of reaching both your business goals and your life goals. But you're going to need help.

Rules of the Hunt is not about miraculous transformation, instant stardom, or life-changing revelations. No book can open a wormhole that allows you to enter and emerge on the other side an entrepreneurial genius, a powerhouse salesperson, or an overnight business sensation. But what this book will do is make your path to business success easier and more enjoyable.

Whether your road to success is a smooth cruise on a four-lane highway or a harrowing ride on an unpaved mountain road has a lot to do with your ability to gain small advantages and avoid mistakes.

Much like winning a game of chess, succeeding in business rarely comes from one brilliant masterstroke. Both winning at chess and succeeding in business come as the result of avoiding errors and gaining an accumulation of small advantages. This book gives you some of those small advantages as well as points out pitfalls to be avoided.

I have strived to keep the writing honest and straightforward. I've written *Rules of the Hunt* for an intelligent yet uninformed friend. You won't find much that's formal or preachy here. You will, despite the occasional cynical comment, find the book to be remarkably optimistic. You'll also find it friendly and easy to read.

Rules of the Hunt has no rigidly structured theme, and my observations, or rules, if you will, vary in density and detail from page to page. Each rule stands on its own and is valuable without reference to another.

This is not a book to be read straight through cover to cover as you might a novel. There is a lot of information on a broad range of subjects. My advice is to read a chapter or two and then take some time to absorb what they contain before going on to the next. You might find it useful to make a few notes as you proceed.

Because *Rules of the Hunt* is not a book of business theory, many of its lessons are valuable to people who are not entrepreneurs. Themes such as leadership, time management, negotiating, and motivating have applications in many different settings.

I don't agree with those who have suggested that I've created a new genre of business book. Despite being markedly different in format and content from other business books, *Rules of the Hunt*, in the end, is simply a book of real-world business advice.

Throughout the book, you'll find practical and sometimes counterintuitive advice along with brief business anecdotes, a few short tutorials, a bit of humor, old-school advice, case histories, an occasional rant, a few horror stories, and some practical suggestions for keeping business in perspective.

Rules of the Hunt covers a broad range of entrepreneurial subjects including leadership, negotiating, motivating people, time management, bartering, recruiting winners, avoiding attorneys, personal growth, sales, marketing, and much more.

You'll find nothing trendy here. There is no theory and no "business religion" to join. *Rules of the Hunt* is simply an honest telling of business experiences and observations.

I acquired this knowledge slowly, and sometimes painfully, through more than three decades of entrepreneurial experience. Having begun my business life with very few advantages, *Rules of the Hunt* is, in some ways, written from the perspective of a business outsider.

I am not at all what you might imagine an entrepreneur to be. I live a modest life centered around my family and home. I have no pretensions of being a high-powered business genius. As a kid who dropped out of high school at age 15 to take a job, I've made a lot of money. But, rags-to-riches stories are common, and this book is not about me.

When I launched my entrepreneurial journey some 30 years ago I was unimaginably ill-prepared. I had no business experience, no money, and very little education. As you might imagine, it was a bumpy ride at first.

Much of what I've learned comes from "in the trenches" experience and is unlikely to ever be part of any business school curriculum. What you'll learn turns conventional "how to become a successful entrepreneur" axioms on their heads.

To survive I became a keenly interested student of human nature, the subtleties of leadership, effective marketing, and the art of selling.

Yes, you'll definitely learn things they won't teach you in business school. I debunk widely held management beliefs, voice my distain for bureaucracies, and wonder aloud why otherwise smart business people hide from their customers.

Some of the ideas and insights in this book will stimulate your imagination, others may inspire you, and a few might make you scratch your head and wonder about my sanity.

I have learned that entrepreneurship is addictive. Like all addictions it can lead to a driven, unbalanced, and obsessive life. Because of this, business success sometimes comes at a terrible personal price. But it doesn't have to be that way. I have devoted a chapter to keeping things in perspective and maintaining your health and sanity. This advice may resemble what you might read in a personal growth book, but what you'll learn will serve you well in surviving your entrepreneurial trek. It's advice I wish had been given to me years ago.

Today innovative computer and communications technology has made becoming your own boss almost unbelievably easy and affordable. Thanks to the Internet, mom-and-pop business operators and would-be kitchen-table tycoons have access to a new universe of minimal-cost-of-entry businesses and markets. With large corporations slashing payrolls, many highly trained and capable employees have been tossed into a dicey job market. The newly unemployed need to work, and many are starting their own businesses. For laid-off or worried workers, launching a business may seem like the best path to survival.

Even though starting a business is now a much more doable and attractive way of making a living than ever before, there is a substantial difference between simply becoming an entrepreneur and becoming a successful entrepreneur.

Even with all the high-tech business tools available to you, you still need a vision, a plan, leadership skills, a keen understanding of human behavior, the willingness to accept responsibility, a knowledge of marketing and sales, daring, and endurance. This book will help you.

When all is said and done, entrepreneurship requires certain personality traits that simply can't be taught; among them are: a deep-seated need to prove your abilities, a high tolerance for risk, and a strong desire for adventure. These attributes are innate, and you won't acquire them by reading this or any other book. However, if you have them, you're halfway home.

To quote one of the best motivational thinkers of our time, Tim Ferriss, "The question you should be asking isn't 'What do I want?' or 'What are my goals?' but 'What would excite me?'"

Find what excites you, and you'll be well on your way to success. When you have reached your goals, I hope you will look back at this book with an appreciation of those small advantages you gained from reading it.

GETTING THE MOST FROM THIS BOOK

Rules of the Hunt contains several hundred rules loosely organized in chapters. Each rule stands on its own without reference to another. The names of the rules do not always correspond to their content. Because of the volume of information and the wide range of subjects covered, you'll find a Directory of Rules at the end of the book. This directory provides space for you to annotate the rules that are of interest to you for quick future reference.

1 THINGS THEY DIDN'T TEACH YOU IN BUSINESS SCHOOL

Formal education will make you a living.
Self-education will make you a fortune.

— JIM ROHN, AMERICAN
ENTREPRENEUR

IN BUSINESS, as in most other walks of life, a good, well-rounded education is a tremendous asset for acquiring success. While there's little question that many business schools provide a very good education, they don't—and can't—deliver a well-rounded one.

Business schools are long, deep, and wide on theory, philosophy, economics, and other "big picture" subjects. This provides a solid foundation for a career in business. But it's not possible for them to give you the experience you will need to deal with the many challenges and opportunities that you'll encounter every day of your business life.

Day-to-day business is firmly rooted in the real world—a world in which one low-profile breakfast can be more productive than a dozen power lunches; a world in which it's often easier to sell something than to give it away; a world in which not being needed can be a very good thing.

Business, especially entrepreneurship, is a brass tacks world that requires having small, but all-important insights, gained only by real-world experience. Here are just a few.

Take responsibility.

The first rule of entrepreneurial success is to take responsibility. Nothing transforms you into a trusted business leader faster than faithfully observing this rule. When you accept complete responsibility for what happens in both your business and your personal life, you transform yourself from participant to director. Once you fully understand and apply this rule, you have already succeeded.

Avoid meetings with more than two or three people.

Meetings are generally a waste of time. The more people in attendance and the longer the meeting lasts, the greater the waste of time. Research shows that many times a meeting's primary purpose is to establish the pecking order within the group. If you must have a meeting, control it. Limit the number of attendees to those absolutely necessary. Have a well-defined agenda and stick to it. Ban cell phones. Start on time. Don't repeat yourself for latecomers. Then get back to work.

There are exceptions to limiting the number of meeting attendees. For example, a brainstorming meeting shouldn't be limited to just two or three people. Be sure to keep brainstorming meetings informal to encourage the free flow of ideas—and limit attendance to fewer than 10 people. The purpose of these meetings is to solve a problem. Once the problem is presented to the group, ideas, even silly ideas, are solicited from attendees and written on a blackboard or some such thing. The ideas are then discussed, and the better ones are adopted. These are by far the most successful and productive kinds of meetings I have attended.

Price can create value.

A friend called me one Saturday afternoon. "I need to ask you a big favor," he began. He explained that he had a family emergency that would take him out of town for several weeks. He asked if I could take a litter of six puppies and give them away to good homes while he was away.

I do love dogs, but I started thinking about the level of care puppies need, and I was about to say no when I heard myself saying, "Sure, why not?" An hour later my friend was at my door with a large bag of Puppy Chow and six very cute and very excited puppies.

Monday morning I placed an ad on a classified advertising site which read: "Cute Australian Shepherd mix puppies. Free." That week I got only four calls and placed just one puppy. Cute as they were, the prospect of continuing to care for five very needful puppies was not pleasant. Then I got an idea.

The following Monday, I posted the same ad with one change. The puppies were no longer free. The price was now $75. To my surprise, the remaining puppies were sold to five happy families within two days.

The lesson of this little story is that price can establish value in the mind of the buyer.

"Steal" good ideas.

When you see a really good marketing concept or packaging innovation, adapt it to your own use. This does not mean that you should plagiarize copy or design. Use concepts only. I used to go to the post office on Saturday mornings and load up on dozens of unopened direct mail pieces that I would "steal" from the waste bins. I would then take them home and analyze them. I got a treasure trove of brilliant ideas from America's leading direct mail experts. You won't find this real-world instruction in any book.

The immutable law of business gift giving.

Women like chocolates and flowers; men like food, gadgets, and toys. Quality trumps quantity. A small box of exquisite chocolate truffles is remembered long after a two-pound box of so-so candy. That's all you need to know.

Don't work more than eight hours a day.

The old entrepreneurial cliché, "I worked fourteen-hour days, six days a week, for five years to build this business," is bunk. If you deduct long lunches, lengthy phone calls, marathon meetings, and bull sessions, this person probably only worked six or seven hours a day. Making the commitment to work an intense eight hours focuses you on priority items, and you'll have more time for friends and family.

When you absolutely must work a few extra hours, do it before office hours. There will be far fewer distractions.

Don't manage for the sake of management.

Most of what we call management consists of making it difficult for people to get their work done. — PETER DRUCKER

Some business owners feel compelled to bring their authority to bear on virtually every project. If your input is necessary, then by all means, give it. If not, get out of the way of your effective and creative people. Your "management" may be slowing them down, and they'll secretly resent it. Overmanagement is a surefire way to lose good people.

Plain English wins the day.

Big words don't equal a bigger brain. Intelligent people who are confident in their message and passionate about what they do don't need obscure language to communicate. — JOHN MCFERRAN, FOUNDER AND PRESIDENT OF PEOPLE FIRST HR SERVICES

Studies show that business communications filled with jargon and "corporate speak" come across as rude, misleading, or obnoxious. Employees and colleagues view simple plain English as honest and friendly. It opens doors and closes deals. Despite this, the business world is awash in pretentious language, jargon, and euphemisms.

"Corporate speak" is the invention of small-minded people who want to avoid responsibility, sound erudite, and sugarcoat the truth. Apparently, it's easier for these clowns to conduct an "exit interview" than to simply fire someone. It's more palatable for them to deal with "personnel displaced inventory" than employee theft, or for equipment to have "deferred maintenance" rather than to simply be run down. My personal favorite is the use of the term "human capital" to describe personnel.

Here are a couple of other examples: "Our platform is a synergistic best-of-breed solution for managing departmental and interpersonal relationships in order to identify and optimally utilize resources." And the head of a major international corporation described the company's ongoing job chopping as, "synergy-related headcount restructuring."

Because it's so commonly used, it's easy to unconsciously let stilted "corporate speak" creep into your business communications. Both customers and investors see a red flag if your language sugarcoats, obscures, misleads, or confuses.

Put simple, honest language to work for you. It's been getting the job done for centuries.

Sometimes it pays to let go.

Take time for all things. —BENJAMIN FRANKLIN

I have a friend who, after working for 20 years in advertising, risked a good deal of his money and went into business for himself. His boutique ad agency was open for several months, but he had not landed a single client. He was working hard: each day he devoted hours to nonstop calling and mailing potential clients. His stress was turning to desperation, and he was a few weeks away from closing his business.

One day, instead of going to work, he stopped at a store and bought a large bag of popcorn. He drove to a park and spent the entire day feeding pigeons, quietly sitting in the sun and watching kids play. He bought a hot dog and lemonade for lunch.

When he got home, his wife asked, "How was your day?" He smiled and said, "Great."

The next day he returned to work to find two inquiries about his services waiting for him. Within a week, both companies were signed. He went on to build a successful business.

Things changed dramatically after his day in the park. Was this the result of his easing his stranglehold on the problem and letting the "law of attraction" work, or did he just get lucky?

It's your call on this one.

Words are powerful and magical things.

Words create impressions, images, and expectations. They build psychological connections. They influence how we think. Since thoughts determine actions, there's a powerful connection between the words we use and the results we get. —NAN S. RUSSELL, FOUNDER AND PRESIDENT OF MOUNTAIN WORKS COMMUNICATIONS

Most successful entrepreneurs understand that they can engage and motivate others by using positive words or powerful imagery. Simply changing or adding a few words to a statement can make it far more compelling. "You will get a full 30 percent discount," blows away, "We are offering a 30 percent discount."

I had to smile when I read the creative imagery of a restaurant menu that offered, not simply "bacon and eggs" but, "Two farm-fresh eggs with country bacon." One description sounds a lot more wholesome and appetizing than the other.

The practice of using positive words and strong imagery helps you achieve better results. This skill is developed simply by understanding and applying it. Use it with business prospects, family, and friends, and you'll begin to reap the rewards.

Intelligence versus wisdom.

I like the humorous observation that intelligence is knowing that a tomato is a fruit while wisdom is knowing not to put it in a fruit salad.

You may be the world's most intelligent person, but this doesn't mean that you have the requisite wisdom to execute every aspect of your business plan. For example, many entrepreneurs think that, because they got straight A's in English literature, they have the talent to write compelling marketing copy. They're wrong.

You would be well advised to seek experienced and talented experts to help you execute the critical aspects of your business and marketing plan.

Look at it this way: Would you rather be lost in the woods with Albert Einstein or Daniel Boone?

Have an interesting story.

Why was Solomon recognized as the wisest man in the world? Because he knew more stories (proverbs) than anyone else. Scratch the surface in a typical boardroom and we're all just cavemen with briefcases, hungry for a wise person to tell us stories. —ALAN KAY, DISNEY FELLOW AT WALT DISNEY IMAGINEERING

You'll make your business more memorable if you have a story with an interesting, entertaining, or surprising element. Publicists call this a "hook." People like a good story, and if you have one, the likelihood of getting publicity increases.

I have an acquaintance who started an auto alarm company. How he developed his theft prevention product makes for an interesting story.

Who would know more about car theft, he reasoned, than car thieves themselves. He located (don't ask me how) several convicted car thieves and learned their tricks and methods for heisting cars. Based on this knowledge, he developed a state-of-the-art product.

Although he never referred to his thief advisors in his advertising, he did use it in his news releases which were widely published in the business press.

Also, consider the story of the second grade teacher who invented an anti-cold supplement, which enhanced the immune system. She invented it, as the story goes, out of self-defense. Her story fires the imagination and conjures up images of second graders sneezing and coughing, filling the air with germs. Her story is one to which buyers can relate.

Remember your excitement and interest as a child when you heard the words, "Once upon a time . . ."? Good stories appeal to the same emotions. A story well told makes your readers feel that they are experiencing it with you.

For stories to work they must identify with the characters. They always want a happy ending.

People rarely remember exactly what you say or do. Their strongest memory of you is how you make them feel. Stories make them feel good.

Imagine that.

Imagination rules the world. — NAPOLEON BONAPARTE

I once served as sales and marketing manager for a start-up trade magazine targeted at the business computing market. It had a huge circulation. Subscriptions were free, and it featured excellent technical articles and product reviews. Our readers loved it. Unfortunately advertisers didn't. This was bad news, of course, since free circulation magazines rely solely on advertising revenues.

Six established magazines were competing for advertising dollars in our market. The crowded field, combined with typical buyer inertia and the fact that we were the new kids on the block, really worked against us.

One morning, while I was thinking about the problem, I had an idea that made me laugh out loud. It was an unusually imaginative idea that I thought just might grab the buyers' attention. It was funny, risky, and a bit bizarre. I liked it.

After identifying the decision makers at 14 of the biggest advertisers in the industry, I assembled the following items:

* Fourteen eight-gallon galvanized garbage pails
* Fourteen bottles of moderately priced champagne
* Ninety-eight crisp one-dollar bills
* A large bag of Styrofoam packing popcorn

Each prospective advertiser was shipped a garbage pail packed with a bottle of champagne and a sales letter with a headline asking, "Are you throwing money away each month?" Spread over the top, were seven crisp one-dollar bills that would be the first things the buyer saw when the garbage pail was opened. I had fun imagining the look on their faces when they lifted the lid.

The enclosed letter invited the buyer to take our challenge. We promised to generate more leads for them than any other industry magazine or their ad would be free. This was exactly the same offer we had been making for several months. It attracted a lot of yawns and only a few advertisers.

The letter went on to explain that the champagne was to celebrate a new and profitable relationship. The letter ended with a PS which read, "The seven dollars we've included are simply to illustrate the point about throwing money away. You might want to brighten a child's day with them."

The results were incredible. Several buyers called to thank us and get more information. The previously disinterested buyers were now enthusiastically taking our calls. The tide was turning. Within 10 days we booked five new advertisers. Another four followed within a few weeks. Within 10 weeks we booked nearly $300,000 in contracted new business. Once the small and medium sized companies saw the big companies advertising, the lemming effect kicked in, and they got onboard.

A year later we were carrying twice the advertising pages of any of our competitors.

Write a headline for your company.

Headlines are really marketing pieces for the accompanying article. They are brief and extract the central idea of a story.

The writer wants to create interest in the article with an intriguing, provocative, or surprising element in the headline.

Often a headline will have humor, a twist, or a play on words.

Headlines are really a form of selling. The headline writer is limited to just a few words to sell the reader the story.

Write a headline about your company that contains humor, a twist, or a play on words. Use no more than seven words. This is an excellent exercise that will help you focus on your core message.

What's your motivation?

My motivation for getting into business was money. Not money to satisfy some narcissistic need for the status symbols of success. I wasn't looking to live in a penthouse suite or to tool down the highway in a high-powered Bugatti. I never dreamed of myself as a celebrated business mogul. I just needed to make money to support my family, and that was motivation enough for me at the time.

So what motivates you?

Do you want independence from a nine-to-five job? Are you in it for the money? Do you just enjoy the creative process? Do you want to pursue a lifelong interest in a business setting? Do you desire the power to influence and control others? Do you have something to prove to yourself? Are you seeking recognition? Do you want the material symbols of success? Or is it a combination of some of these things?

It's good to know what your motivation is because your reasons for entering business will be a major factor in not only identifying the product or service you provide but also in defining your overall goal as well. It is easier to attain what you want if you clearly define your motivation.

Creating the "gotta have it."

Give a man a fish and he will eat for a day. Teach a man to fish and he will eat for a lifetime. Teach a man to create an artificial shortage of fish and he will eat steak. —JAY LENO

That which is difficult to attain is more valuable than that which is easily acquired.

I'm talking about creating demand by intentionally limiting supply.

Women who play hard-to-get understand this well. The desire to possess something increases with the lack of its availability.

This hard-wired human behavioral trait is demonstrated nearly every Christmas season. A toy manufacturer introduces a "must-have" toy that quickly sells out at full retail price. People then wait anxiously and line up to buy it when the shelves are restocked. After all, who knows when it will be available again?

This same phenomenon is seen with personal electronics. A phone manufacturer has a highly publicized product release. The publicity is so effective that prerelease orders are being booked by retailers. That cool phone becomes unavailable shortly after it is released. New back orders keep coming. By throttling back supply, the manufacturer creates demand.

Manufacturers intentionally create these shortages to cash in on the power of the "gotta have it."

An extreme example involves the Volkswagen Beetle. Shortly after it was introduced, the Beetle was so wildly popular that some dealerships displayed the cars on their showroom floors with locked doors. You couldn't sit in one, and test drives were out of the question. You paid full price or you didn't get one.

An even more extreme example is the Beverly Hills caterer who charges twice as much as his competitors and is booked months in advance. If you want to hire him, you must be referred by someone who knows him. He has an unlisted phone number!

Write your dream plan.

There is a theory about a phenomenon to which I subscribe. It states that once a thought is committed to writing, it becomes manifest.

Start writing a book on the story of how and why your business was started. Give it a title. You don't need to spend a lot of time on this. You need to write only the first two paragraphs. Outline a table of contents with year-by-year chapter headings. Include the milestones in the growth of your business and when they were reached. Be optimistic and perhaps a bit fanciful. Write the final paragraph summarizing your company's happy ending. Save what you have written.

This is, of course, not a business plan but an exercise in dreaming. You have to have a dream in order for it to come true.

Hire traits, not degrees.

The fact that a job applicant has a degree doesn't reveal much about that candidate's capabilities.

Many people who hold advanced degrees lack common sense.

The Wizard of Oz couldn't give the Scarecrow brains, but he could give him a diploma. Lots of incompetents have diplomas. Don't be too impressed by these.

Honesty, loyalty, initiative, and dedication can't be taught. The real world of business requires traits and abilities that are not attained by simply having a degree.

2 | LEADERSHIP

The art of communication is the language of leadership. —James Humes, American lawyer, speaker, and author

LEADERSHIP IS A complex subject that has been the topic of countless books. Opinions vary widely on what it takes to lead. What I have learned about leadership is that the difference between running a company and running the rest of your life isn't all that big.

The old military command and control style of leadership doesn't work in a business environment. However, like a military leader, a business leader must clearly communicate the "mission." Note that I find the word *mission* too broad and a bit nebulous. *Destination* is a more useful word; you can't lead without a clear destination.

Leadership has as much to do with who you aren't as it does with who you are. I have found, with few exceptions, that excellent leaders are also good people. They are empathetic, honest, responsible, unpretentious, plain-spoken, and focused, and they set positive examples. Beyond these attributes there is the mixture of two essential elements that fuel successful leadership: communication and passion. Communicating the team goal with passion is the key. I'm not talking about fiery speeches or contrived pep rallies. I'm talking about continually showing your passionate commitment to reaching the destination, not only with words, but with actions. My advice is that if you're not passionate about what you are doing, find something that you do feel passionate about.

This chapter offers some very powerful leadership secrets, but it can't give you your passion.

Don't tell people what to do; tell them who they are.

The most subtle and powerful rule you'll ever learn for motivating people is to tell them who they are rather than telling them what to do.

Example: You're at the DMV, and you approach the clerk with an exasperated expression. You sigh and say, "This form is confusing; I can't figure it out." The clerk looks at you disdainfully and advises you to read the instructions on the reverse of the form, looks past you, and says, "Next."

Now imagine approaching the same clerk with the same problem. This time, however, you approach her with a smile and say, "You look like the person who can answer a couple of questions for me about this form."

The clerk smiles back and says, "Let's see what you've got here," and quickly answers your questions.

In the first example it's all about you and your problem. In the second example it's all about the clerk. You began your request by telling her who she is by acknowledging her as an expert with the knowledge that can help you. She immediately wants to prove you right and she does.

The same approach works equally well with employees and vendors.

Example: You call an employee into your office and say, "I need you to get this report finalized. I need it by next Friday."

The employee sighs and resignedly says, "Okay."

If, however, you were to say, "Jeanette, you came to mind immediately as the perfect person to get this report finalized."

Jeanette smiles and says, "I'll do my best."

Just as in the first example, your initial statement was again all about you and your needs. In the second, you acknowledged Jeanette's competence and professionalism and expressed confidence in her abilities. She will work hard to prove you right.

An extreme example: A few years back, I hired a young woman to do research for the company. She was well qualified and had specific experience in the area of marketing research for which she was hired. Although she was painfully shy, her shyness did not affect her work. Things changed when her duties expanded, and she was required to talk with vendors and affiliates. Her shyness was a big impediment to one-on-one communication, and she told me so. She seemed ready to resign when we spoke.

While thinking about the problem, I reviewed her résumé and noted in the "personal interests" section that she participated in local theater. The next day, I asked her to drop by my office. I asked her how a person as shy as she was able to go on stage before a live audience. She told me that it was different because she was simply playing a character on stage. Once she was on stage, she told me, her shyness disappeared.

I decided to try an experiment. That evening, I rewrote her résumé. Her new résumé gave her a new personality and number of attributes that she did not possess.

Her résumé now identified her as a motivational speaker and personal coach. I even changed her name and gave her a slightly different age, as well as a different place of birth. She was now a Southern girl from the tony hamlet of Biltmore Forest, North Carolina.

The next day, I called her into the office, and asked her if she would be willing to participate in an experiment. I asked her if she would take a new name and play a role whenever she was at the office. She looked at me quizzically.

I handed her the résumé and asked if she could play the person described in the résumé and consider the office her stage. As she read it, she slowly smiled and then looked up and said, "I can do this."

The following day, there was a noticeable difference. Her shyness seemed to be replaced by a quiet confidence. In the coming week, I noticed changes in the way she dressed and carried herself. Although she never became really outgoing, she had no problem talking with our business partners. She played her role well.

This is obviously an extreme example and requires a special personality type. I don't suggest you try it, but it does illustrate the point.

Leading the pack.

Talent wins games, but teamwork and intelligence wins championships. — Michael Jordan

Leading a team is complex. The more team members there are, the greater the complexity.

Besides money, team members want recognition, praise, respect, and to work with a well-defined plan. People want to be part of a team that is well-led and successful. They want to feel that they have contributed to the success of the team. They want to belong.

There is a very strong relationship between team happiness and satisfaction and your bottom line.

There are many excellent learning resources to help you understand team dynamics and sharpen your leadership skills. Educate yourself.

Always remember that the quality of your leadership is the primary influence on how your team behaves and performs.

Instruction whispers; example screams.

Example is not the main thing in influencing others. It is the only thing. —ALBERT SCHWEITZER

You set an example by looking, acting, and thinking like a leader. Work as hard, or harder, than your team members. You set a powerful example by occasionally rolling your sleeves up and getting your hands dirty. Staying at the rear of the battle is not inspiring and sets a bad example. Leading the charge says in the most dramatic way, "I'm your leader. Follow me."

Keep your cool. Respond calmly to those big challenges that are sure to come your way. While you can't know what specific problem will come knocking, you can anticipate how you react to it. A calm response is a strong example of your leadership skills, which will not be lost on others.

Develop first-rate communication skills. Never sugarcoat a problem or deliver an unclear directive. Tell it like it is. People are not afraid of the truth and will readily follow a leader who is direct. When you are honest, realistic, and plain spoken, you'll avoid misunderstandings and mistakes. A straightforward communication style is the hallmark of good leadership. Clarify, prioritize, and lead.

The less detailed, the more empowering.

During World War II, Franklin D. Roosevelt sent General Dwight D. Eisenhower instructions for joining the war in Europe. These instructions were limited to seven simple words: "Seek out the enemy and destroy him." Specific details on how to accomplish this goal were not included. Roosevelt's message made it clear that he deemed General Eisenhower competent to wage war and fully empowered him to do so.

In business, if you are dealing with an experienced and competent associate, abbreviated instructions will sometimes get you the results you are looking for because they also empower the recipient.

Who's in charge here?

The one in charge is both optimistic and industrious. This person is aware and not easily fooled and has the contradictory personality traits of daring and caution. This is a serious but fun-loving individual who enjoys challenges. This person is empathetic and adept at reading and motivating people. This practical person is also a dreamer and has both a vision and a plan.

Keep your word.

Your word is all you have. Few things send a more negative message to others than your failing to keep a commitment. Failure to deliver, even on seemingly insignificant agreements, is bad business and bad leadership.

Don't make commitments casually. Just as you wouldn't sign a check without money in the bank to cover it, don't make commitments when you have insufficient time to keep them. If you are unsure that you will be able to keep an agreement, it's better to say something like, "I will try to have it to you by Friday, but no promises." Be realistic when you're making a commitment.

It doesn't matter if you have an excuse. A commitment is both a promise and a contract. Neither can be broken with an excuse.

You'll make commitments every day. It's an inescapable part of doing business. Some are small, while others seem bigger and more important. The truth is that whether large or small, a commitment is a commitment, and all should be viewed as equally important.

Not keeping your word breaks trust and diminishes your reputation and credibility. If you can't deliver, contact the other party early. This person will respect your integrity and thoughtfulness. Depending on the urgency of the matter, most people happily accommodate a change in plans. The key is to make the contact early. A call 20 minutes before a meeting saying you can't make it is a broken commitment.

Things run more smoothly when commitments are thoughtfully made and unfailingly kept. Your reliability, or lack thereof, never goes unnoticed by friends, family, customers, and business associates.

Master the art of delegation.

The first rule of management is delegation. Don't try to do everything yourself because you can't. —ANTHEA TURNER, BRITISH TELEVISION PERSONALITY

You'll accelerate the growth of your business if you learn to delegate.

I asked one CEO at a small company, who was spending hours on a tedious bookkeeping chore, why he didn't hire temporary help to come in and do it. He replied, "Temps cost money."

His attempt at saving money by doing clerical work himself was a false economy of the first order. Instead of using his time doing the things that would grow his business, he had, I suspect, found a way to avoid real responsibility by creating a "must do" job for himself.

Entrepreneurs can quickly get swamped by attempting to micromanage every aspect of their business. It is essential to allow others to help.

Owners of successful enterprises have learned to delegate and let go of tasks others can do so that they can concentrate on driving growth.

Confront problems early.

Confronting problems when they occur is a sign of good leadership. It's rarely a good strategy to wait for things to get better and hope they eventually work themselves out.

Problems feed on procrastination and fear. Hit problems between the eyes as soon as they show themselves, because little problems have a way of becoming big problems if they are left unattended.

If you don't take action, your ability to lead will be questioned. Furthermore, team members will become discouraged if they see problems go unaddressed.

It may be an annoying distraction to handle a problem right away. In fact, confronting a problem head on may be downright unpleasant, but it is better to act and not allow a problem to linger and grow bigger.

Know when to look the other way.

During the Civil War, Abraham Lincoln, when informed of Ulysses Grant's heavy drinking, reportedly requested that someone find out what Grant was drinking and send it to each of the other generals.

Lincoln looked the other way because Grant was getting the job done.

Sometimes in business it pays to look away. You may have a wise-cracking sales manager who is loud and obnoxious. His personality is annoying, but he shines at bringing new business to your company.

It's not what you say; it's how you say it!

Words are, of course, the most powerful drug used by mankind.
— RUDYARD KIPLING

Persuasive speakers communicate by using positive language. For example, instead of saying, "We can't ship your order until next Tuesday," say, "We can ship your order as early as next Tuesday." What a difference! Put yourself in the listener's shoes. Which version is more appealing? The habit of using positive speech has helped me to achieve more than I ever thought possible. You can practice this skill all the time, too. Try it with coworkers, family members, and friends. You'll begin to see things in a whole new light!

Meet the members of the cast.

Over the years I have attended and conducted countless meetings. I have observed that certain personality types seem to make an appearance at meetings of any size. See if you recognize any.

The *Magpie* can't stop talking to everyone around him. The Magpie is oblivious to what is being said and is often talking while the meeting leader is speaking. I try to control the Magpie by stopping and asking the Magpie to share what he is saying with the rest of the group. Don't put him on the spot. Do this with a friendly smile. This approach buys five or ten minutes of meeting time until once again the urge to talk is too great to bear and the Magpie starts to chatter again.

The *Sharpshooter* wants to establish himself as the smartest person in the room by making others wrong. Sharpshooters are adept at asking questions that they believe are beyond the knowledge of the speaker or the team.

The *Bomb Thrower* waits for an opportune time to introduce an inflammatory opinion designed to send shockwaves through the group.

The *Bobblehead* agrees. Usually you'll end up with several Bobbleheads in the room. They avoid any real participation by enthusiastically agreeing with everything that is said. Their heads never seem to stop nodding.

The *Sphinx* is silent and expressionless. It's hard to figure out what the Sphinx is thinking. I usually ask, "What are your thoughts?" to encourage his participation.

The *Clown* loves to interject comic observations and ask questions designed to elicit laughter. This attention-getting behavior is covert hostility.

The *Orator* gets the floor and she is off and running. Attendees will get a speech worthy of the most verbose political candidate. Often the Orator starts with a laundry list of reasons why the problem needs to be addressed. Next comes a recounting of a similar problem that perhaps occurred at a previous place of employment. The Orator seeks to establish her expertise on the subject. No detail is left out. Listeners learn the names, and sometimes the personality traits, of those who worked with her in the past in solving the problem. Relax and take a deep breath. Wait for the opportune time to get the meeting back on track.

The *Complexifier* is well-meaning but annoying. The first words out of the Complexifier's mouth are, "Yes but . . ." This is followed by his pointing out a problem that would arise by taking the action being discussed. Even if told the problem has been considered and a solution found, the next words spoken by the Complexifier are, "Yes but . . ." Be patient because, on rare occasions, the Complexifier does point out an unwanted outcome that has not been considered.

Keep it real.

Be yourself; everyone else is already taken. — OSCAR WILDE

Don't try to be someone you are not. It will be a painful experience for both you and the person you are trying to mislead. Do what you do well. Be who you are, and you will not only be authentic, but you will get respect and have far greater persuasive power in business.

In 1776 Benjamin Franklin was named ambassador to France. Instead of trying to fit in with the powdered wig crowd, Franklin wore a fur cap and homespun clothing. He refused to join the social masquerade and understood that the French would appreciate authenticity. He was right. He was the toast of Paris.

The good, the bad, and the ugly.

Some people don't need to be led. They are completely onboard, know the goals, and have rolled their sleeves up and are hard at work. Others are difficult to lead. These people may lack the confidence to perform what is being asked of them, or they may have issues with authority and being directed. Then there are those who can't be led. These people may consider themselves separate from the team. They do not respect the leader and are often disdainful of his or her decisions. They are remarkably uninterested in the team goals and resent any attempt to be led. They won't be with your organization for long.

Get rid of marginal personnel quickly.

The old business adage, "Be slow to hire and quick to fire," is usually good advice.

You will know, probably within a month or so, whether you've made a hiring mistake. Recognize your error early on and correct it. While firing someone is unpleasant for both parties, it's a necessary job that you must occasionally do in order to succeed. It's a job that shouldn't be delegated.

However, if you are firing people too often, something is wrong. If you are devoting a lot of your time correcting bad hiring decisions, it is time to rethink your hiring practices.

It's easy to find yourself squandering precious time and energy dealing with hiring and firing instead of growing your business. In addition to the time and energy wasted, your momentum is slowed, and there is, of course, lost production and the expense of recruiting and training a replacement.

The quality of those you hire will go a long way toward determining your success. Get the help and training you need to professionalize your hiring processes. It is time well spent.

Nobody is at fault.

When you are faced with firing someone, avoid accusations. No matter how badly someone has screwed things up, never mention it. Let this person out gently. Remember, you hired this employee so in the end, it really is your fault. I always tell people before I hire them that we are both on a 90-day mutual probation. If for any reason they don't like the job, I encourage them to tell me. No specific reason need be given. I reserve the right to terminate their employment in the 90-day period under the same conditions. (Employment laws differ from state to state. Make certain it's legal to enter into such an agreement in your state.)

Expect the unexpected.

A Scout is never taken by surprise; he knows exactly what to do when anything unexpected happens. — ROBERT BADEN-POWELL, FOUNDER OF THE BOY SCOUT MOVEMENT

I worked for the Forest Service one summer, and I remember a poster on the wall of the vehicle bay that showed a truck rounding a curve with a Big Foot crossing the road. It was emblazoned, "Expect the Unexpected."

While the poster was funny, the message was serious. Anyone driving a truck on a mountain road needs to expect the unexpected.

The same goes for business. You never expected that key person to quit without notice at the peak of your busy season. The unexpected is not always bad. Who could have predicted that a huge unsolicited order would come in from a big national company?

The unforeseen is unavoidable, but being psychologically prepared when it comes knocking goes a long way toward removing panic and anger from the event.

With this expectation comes the confidence that you are aware of the possibility and ready to deal with any unexpected contingency.

Enthusiasm is contagious.

Catch on fire with enthusiasm and people will come for miles to watch you burn. — JOHN WESLEY, ENGLISH PREACHER AND FOUNDER OF THE METHODIST MOVEMENT

I worked with a firm whose marketing manager would yell, "Yes!!" or, "Sweet!!" every time an order came in over the Internet. The larger the order, the louder he would yell. He would sometimes emerge from his office to excitedly announce the details. As undignified as this may seem, his reaction amused and excited the members of his team, and their work reflected this. They were having fun. You don't have to yell, but your excitement about your company's progress, plans, prospects, and product sends an irresistible message to customers and employees alike.

Handle difficult situations yourself.

Never delegate what is difficult. The resolution of tough problems is your job. This includes unpleasant tasks such as dealing with an angry customer or tackling difficult negotiations. By taking on the hard situations yourself, you demonstrate strong leadership qualities to those around you. Perhaps more importantly, you're more likely to get the results you want.

Discourage nonanswers.

I was gratified to be able to answer promptly, and I did. I said I didn't know.   — MARK TWAIN

Nonanswers are purposely vague and are given to obscure, sugarcoat, or avoid taking responsibility. They convey little or no useful information.

Politicians have nonanswers down to a science. They are experts at answering tough questions by artfully avoiding anything resembling an appropriate answer. Watch a political debate, and you'll see the art of the nonanswer as it is performed by the pros.

The practice, of course, is not limited to waffling politicians. Many people regularly give nonresponsive answers. For example, imagine your frustration if you asked a doctor the extent of the injuries your skiing partner received in an accident and the reply was, "She took a pretty bad fall."

Nonanswers are common in the workplace. If you ask an employee who is managing a mailing project, "Will we get the mailing out on October 1?" a nonanswer would be, "We should be in pretty good shape." This is a watered down yes—an element of uncertainty is the word *should*.

An answer that's actually an answer would be, "I just checked with the printer and the mail house, and the job is on schedule." An even better response would be if, "I'll stay on it and keep you posted," was added. It would also be a perfectly good response if he or she said, "I don't know. Let me check and I'll get back to you."

As a leader you should recognize nonanswers and respond to them by explaining why nonanswers are not an acceptable way of communicating in business.

Personally read all complaint letters.

Reading all complaint letters yourself can be very instructive. Perhaps you will identify an area in your product or customer service that needs to be improved. On the other hand, remember that you will also get your share of unwarranted complaints from people who have nothing better to do with their time than write letters.

Set unreasonably high goals for yourself.

I subscribe to Fred Bucy's (former president and CEO of Texas Instruments) law which states, "Nothing is ever accomplished by a reasonable man." Become unreasonable, come on strong in this area, and have seemingly unattainable dreams. Real progress often depends on unreasonable people.

Are your goals unreasonable?

Lavish praise.

I like to praise and reward loudly, to blame quietly. — CATHERINE II

Giving praise when praise is due inspires loyalty. People want to be heroes; as a leader, you have the power to make them so. The more public the praise, the greater its impact. Always make certain that the praise is deserved. Flattery is seen as manipulative, and it is easily seen through. Praise is especially effective when the person being praised believes you think he or she is out of earshot.

Communicate with grace.

Communication works for those who work at it.

— JOHN POWELL, MOTION PICTURE
SCORE COMPOSER

People are easily offended. Take care to avoid using words or phrases around employees and business associates that might offend or be misconstrued.

Risqué jokes and off-color language may be funny to some, but you should avoid them, along with other taboo topics.

I once worked with a company whose CEO used colorful language. During a staff meeting I attended, he said, "We'll have a 'Come to Jesus' meeting with them," by which he meant a meeting to give those in attendance a keen understanding of the reality of their situation.

One of his key people, a devout Christian, quit her job the next day because she found the expression sacrilegious. It wasn't the first time she had heard him use the expression. She had asked him to not use this phrase several times, but it was a handy phrase he used probably unconsciously.

Such phrases should be carefully avoided in a business setting.

Similar missteps can occur when gift giving. I know of one firm that sent expensive bottles of 18-year-old Scotch to the executives of a client firm in Utah. All the executives were church-going Mormons. The client sent back the Scotch with a note that read: "Thanks for thinking of us, but we have no use for this gift."

Imagine the embarrassment of another business owner in the midwest when he learned that the firm in New York to which he had sent an expensive smoked ham was owned and operated by Orthodox Jews.

Use power with restraint.

Diplomacy: the art of restraining power. — HENRY A. KISSINGER

In an election, everyone's vote counts. Businesses, however, are not democracies. Some votes carry more weight than others. In fact, if it's your company, in the end, it's only your vote that matters. It's important that you use this power with restraint.

If you have a policy, state the reason for the policy. I have known many managers who had a "because I said so" attitude. I actually heard one manager say, "This is a business, not a debating society" when an employee asked the reason for a policy. This is a childish and all-too-common abuse of power that creates resentment and can drive talented people away.

Dismissing a team member's idea without discussion also leads to resentment and negativity. A team member may be angered if an idea is rejected without discussion. It is unlikely that this person will present an idea to you again. The idea, had you examined and discussed it, may have had merit.

A smart leader understands power and listens with respect and restraint.

Don't make me come back there!

Avoid refereeing power struggles within your organization. Such conflicts are usually about the combatants' place in the hierarchy. If you can, let the two parties work it out. If it accelerates to the point to where it is distracting others or slowing down work, then and only then is it time for you to mediate the battle. Try to come up with a solution that both parties dislike.

Invite criticism.

O would some power the gift to give us to see ourselves as others see us.
— ROBERT BURNS

When egos are involved, it is difficult to look at a project, plan, or even an idea critically.

Accepting criticism from others is hard to do. It's a natural reaction to become defensive when we are criticized. Sometimes it causes resentment or even provokes a counterattack.

I view criticism differently. I think it is valuable. The more honest it is, the more valuable it is. I don't want cheerleaders. I want unvarnished opinion, as critical, blunt, and insensitive as it needs to be. You can't hurt my feelings. This is business. Pull no punches. Nothing sugarcoated, please.

Criticism is needed in order to learn, rethink, grow, and improve. Encourage it.

Value the power of silence.

I sometimes respond to people who have just given me a bit of gossip by remaining silent. Within a few seconds, they realize that my silence means that I do not want to pursue the subject with them. I didn't tell them that—my silence did.

In some cultures, silence is a sign of respect. If one is asked a question in these cultures, it is expected that a period of silence will elapse while the question is contemplated before an answer is given.

Silence has a mysterious effect. It has the power to get people to act. It can help slow the mind so that decisions can be made. It can be a powerful ally or enemy. It is a force with many uses.

Silence is also a powerful negotiating tool. When the person you're negotiating with puts the proposal on the table or proposes a deal, your remaining silent quickly has him or her rethinking the offer.

A friend of mine, who was on the management team of a Canadian publishing company, recalls a business meeting where silence had an unexpected effect. The management team was meeting with a software vendor who had given a product demo and answered questions. When he quoted his price, the group fell silent. This was not a negotiating tactic, but the price was far lower than they had budgeted for. They were all secretly smiling inside but didn't utter a word. After five seconds of silence, the vendor said, "Okay, okay, how about if I lower the price by 10 percent?" The team was shocked and quickly accepted the offer. Not only did the software vendor lose 10 percent, but he also lost some respect.

Winners have something to prove.

I think that successful people have something to prove. They love playing the game, and they want to win. Winning is more important to them than the money that comes with it. In the words of my friend and mentor Jim Armstrong, "Money is just a way of keeping score—the points on the board."

Use the power of "no."

There are occasions where saying no is the best time management practice there is. —CATHERINE PULSIFER, INSPIRATIONAL WRITER

No is an extremely useful and powerful word. The fewer the exclamation points following it, the greater its power.

Whether negotiating or responding to an unreasonable request, a simple, quietly spoken no indicates your complete understanding of what is being asked and suggests that you have already given some thought to the matter and have made your decision.

The most important person you should learn to say no to is yourself.

Don't hide from your employees.

Have an open-door policy both figuratively and literally.

This advice sounds almost silly; however, I have met many business owners who kept an unreasonable distance between themselves and their employees. These folks were usually hard workers who simply did not want to be distracted. I believe you should have an open-door policy, both in theory and in practice. Nobody likes to knock on the boss's office door. Make it unnecessary.

A closed door is often construed in a negative way. Let your employees know you are accessible and are always ready to listen when they have ideas or concerns. Being available to employees shows good leadership.

Be friendly, but don't make friends with your employees.

I have learned that you get the best team results if you maintain psychological distance between yourself and your employees. The problem with being friends with an employee is that it changes the context of your relationship. The old saying, "Familiarity breeds contempt" contains a lot of truth.

Take employees to a business lunch, but never have an after-work drink with them. Never invite employees to your home unless you want them to learn what is in your medicine cabinet.

Keep it friendly, but keep it business.

Stay curious.

The important thing is not to stop questioning. Curiosity has its own reason for existing. —ALBERT EINSTEIN

Most of the really successful businesspeople I know are remarkably curious. They ask thoughtful and penetrating questions: "How does that work?" "What is your evidence for that?" "Why do you think that happens in the way it does?"

Curiosity is a sign of intelligence. It creates a state of constant learning, and learning new things leads to success.

Practice creative rule breaking.

Hell, there are no rules here—we're trying to accomplish something.
—THOMAS A. EDISON

I like upsetting the status quo by breaking a few rules and trying new ideas. I've always had an innate dislike of rules as they apply to building a business.

The status quo is the foundation of that gray citadel where mediocrity resides.

Most of the world's great accomplishments were made by those who broke the rules. Every great business idea in some way breaks a rule.

The most dismal utterance is, "We've always done it that way."

Many rules are made to be broken. The secret is to know which ones to break and when to break them.

When you start your own business, don't follow the safe, beaten path. Blaze your own trail. Break a few rules.

All you need to know about leadership.

A good objective of leadership is to help those who are doing poorly to do well and to help those who are doing well to do even better.

— JIM ROHN, AMERICAN
ENTREPRENEUR

Be the leader. It's your agenda. It's your business. It's your dream. It's your responsibility. Focus on the goals. Share your vision. Be kind. Communicate clearly. Do the work. Get things done, and get them done today. Maintain your integrity. Set the example. Leave excuses at the door.

3 | RELATIONSHIPS

RELATIONSHIPS AND PLANTS both need care and watering. The quality of your relationships with employees, customers, and vendors has a direct bearing on the vitality and profitability of your enterprise.

If you are a "people person," relationships will come easily. However, if you aren't, there's still hope for you because relationship-building skills can be learned. Your ability to deal well with people will grow as you become successful. Let it come naturally. Trying to be charming or outgoing will come off as inauthentic and will retard rather than accelerate the growth of a relationship.

Don't worry if you are not irresistibly magnetic. Simply being likable is enough to build strong relationships. If you take an interest in people, they will like you, and a relationship is the natural result. Renowned motivational expert Dale Carnegie said it best, "You can make more friends in two months by becoming truly interested in other people than you can in two years by trying to get other people interested in you."

Three people you should take to lunch.

Invite your banker to lunch. It's best to do this when you don't need financial services and just want to introduce yourself. Have a friendly conversation. Tell her about your company and your long-term goals. Bankers are great sources of referrals and introductions. They meet a lot of businesspeople. Once they know you, they may send someone in need of your product or service. If the time comes when you do need a loan or a bank reference, you have the inside track.

Take the head of your largest supplier to lunch. Talk shop and learn what's new. Talk about your business goals and subtly let him know your value as a customer. The main reason for this lunch is that if you ever have a problem with price, delivery, or any of the many other things that can go wrong with a supplier, you'll get a much quicker and satisfactory resolution if you are friends with the CEO.

Take your competitor to lunch. This isn't as crazy as it may seem. You'll be surprised by how much you will learn when talking over lunch. The reasons for your getting together are to demystify the competition, get a feel for its management, and create a collegial relationship.

Of the dozen or so competitors I've invited to lunch over the years, only a few have been hostile and refused the invitation. I think many accepted my invitation out of curiosity, and a few seemed genuinely flattered. If the competitor is not local, arrange for a lunch or dinner when you are both at a trade show, exhibition, or conference.

Competition doesn't always have to be unpleasant or adversarial. I've had competitors, who, because they knew and liked me, referred customers to me when they were backlogged or weren't set up to handle the client's needs.

Part as friends.

When the time comes, it's important that you terminate your relationships with vendors and other business partners with professionalism and grace. The reason, of course, is you want to maintain some degree of a relationship even though you are no longer doing business. This professional courtesy shows good business form. You never know when you may need their services again.

Acquire champions.

Skill is fine, and genius is splendid, but the right contacts are more valuable than either. —Arthur Conan Doyle

Establish relationships with people like you and who are enthusiastic about what you are doing. This can be almost anybody from your barber to your banker. Champions are a wonderful source of referrals and can expand your business network. If you are dealing with a large, bureaucratic organization, having a champion within that company really pays dividends. Find one.

Be inclusive, not exclusive. Imagine having several hundred advocates, some in very high places, who champion your business. This group should include friends, family, vendors, employees, and customers.

Pick up your pen.

My uncle, who was in sales all his life, was married to my aunt for nearly 50 years. Theirs was that rare romantic storybook marriage based on mutual respect and affection.

My uncle had an endearing habit that I'm sure contributed to their successful marriage. Once or twice a week, before going to work, he would leave a few handwritten notes around their home in places where he was sure my aunt would find them. They were simple one-line messages like, "I'm looking forward to this evening with you" or "I'm so glad you're my wife." Years after his death my aunt still remembered his notes and spoke of them often.

Today, with so many quick and inexpensive ways to communicate electronically, handwritten business notes are becoming rare.

A handwritten note says to the recipient: this is from a human being. It has impact because it connects on a human level in a way that cannot be matched by any other means.

You can be sure that, unlike an e-mail, your note will be opened and read.

Never send one with a business message or a call to action. A handwritten note should be brief and used to congratulate or thank someone or to just say hello. It will be opened, and you will be remembered.

Let's not do lunch.

You'll get more done over a breakfast meeting than you will at lunch or dinner. The ideas discussed at a breakfast have a greater chance of being implemented that day rather than those discussed at the later lunch and even later dinner.

Lunches are the second choice, but since they occur midday, peoples' energy and attention, to some degree, are winding down, especially after the meal is finished.

A business dinner is excellent if it is strictly a social event. It's far more difficult to stick to an agenda at a business dinner because dinner is associated with end-of-the-day leisure, and alcohol is often consumed.

You can call me Mike.

Formality in business communications is slowly becoming extinct. Increasingly, business letters, especially those sent electronically, do not use the recipient's last name in the salutation. "Hello Bob" has replaced "Dear Mr. Smith."

In my view this is a good thing. I have long opted for informality in my letters because it's friendlier and is more likely to engage the reader. Of course, if the recipient of your letter has a professional title, don't neglect to use it.

It's worth noting that some cultures view informality in business as a sign of disrespect. Make sure you've done your homework.

Today's informality extends to clothing. If you go casual, make sure your clothes are of high quality (that means expensive) and well fitting. A young Bill Gates, as the legend goes, got one of the best business deals in history pitching a group of IBM executives in gray flannel suits while wearing torn Levi's and a T-shirt. While jeans may not have held back Bill, he also just happened to be offering a revolutionary product.

You make a better impression with most people if you are sharply dressed.

Take a lesson from your best friend.

Dogs and philosophers do the greatest good and get the fewest rewards.
— Diogenes

Dogs can teach a lesson to anyone in business.

Canines came in from the wild many millennia ago. They are the oldest domesticated animal and one of the most common household pets. These intelligent creatures brought with them huge benefits for humanity. The many jobs dogs perform for us is mind-boggling. They are guards, rescuers, herders, entertainers, guides, therapists, crime fighters, and much more.

Above all, dogs are skilled entrepreneurs who have mastered the arts of communication, persuasion, and selling.

Like any good businessperson, dogs are honest. There is not much chance of misunderstanding them. Happy, angry, wary, hungry, or on the alert, they let you know their state of mind.

Like successful businesspeople, dogs know how to ask for what they want. It's a job they do with great expertise. While dogs can't speak, they do tell us their needs via body language that's easy to understand.

Dogs understand how to engage. Their sincere excitement about and interest in their business partner (that would be you) is flattery on a level that's hard to resist. Whenever you are greeted by your dog, it's easy to understand the famous quote, sometimes attributed to Mark Twain, "My goal in life is to be as good a person as my dog thinks I am."

Do talk to strangers.

Good things happen when you meet strangers. —Yo-Yo Ma

Talk to strangers? Bad advice for a kid, but good for an entrepreneur. I find that engaging in conversation with strangers is both educational and fun. I've turned it into something of a game. I engage others whenever there's an opportunity. Whether paying a parking attendant or waiting in a doctor's office, if I see an opportunity, I take it. I am occasionally met with a dismissive grunt, but most people are very approachable, and it doesn't take much to get them talking.

I was waiting in a checkout line at a small country store near my home. An older woman was checking out her groceries in front of me. She had some interesting food items. I smiled and said, "I wish I was having dinner at your house."

She immediately lit up and described a Greek dish she was making that evening. She added that it was her husband's favorite.

I saw her again in the parking lot as she was loading her groceries. She was parked a few cars away from mine. As I passed, I said, "Let me help you with those."

She liked to talk. She told me about her son, who was a doctor. She even mentioned she was married in 1962 in New Hampshire. The conversation was interesting but a bit one-sided.

I finally found an opening to gracefully break off and said, "Enjoy that Greek dish!"

As I started to walk away, she surprised me by asking if my wife and I would join her and her husband for dinner.

I said, "No, we couldn't do that."

She smiled and said, "Sure you could."

After 10 minutes, I ended up accepting her invitation and later had fun explaining to my wife how it came to be that we were having dinner at a stranger's home.

We were warmly greeted at the door by both her and her husband. Her husband, who was an architect, showed a real interest in me. He asked a lot of questions and shared stories from his military and business experiences. His wife, who had taught music at a university, played piano with my wife.

My small kindness led to a memorable evening, and I was privileged to get a view into the lives of those interesting and accomplished people.

Another time, while standing in line for a cup of coffee in a crowded and noisy shop, I said to a man in line with me, "There sure is no recession here!" He smiled and said a little wistfully, "I wish I could say the same for my business." He went on to tell me how once robust sales at his company had all but dried up. As we neared the cash register, I asked for his business card and told him I would send him my sales book on ways to beat the downturn.

As promised, I sent him the book and received a thank you note by return mail. A couple of weeks later he placed an order for 40 copies of the book for his team.

I met Oscar in an unusual way. He was my server at a Chinese restaurant. He was a confident, well-spoken young man with an engaging manner. He suggested that I try a special dish for dinner; I decided to follow his recommendation. When he brought the food to the table, I asked if he was in college. He seemed a little surprised by the question and asked, "How did you know?" I told him that he looked like a college student. I learned that he was a business student majoring in marketing. When I told him I was in marketing, he began to ask questions.

The restaurant was closing, and I gave him my business card and invited him to call me anytime. To my surprise he did call. I was impressed that he asked real how-to questions.

His questions were the kind of "nuts and bolts" questions a person about to launch a business might ask. I learned that he was indeed starting his own business while he continued his education. During his start-up he would call me at least once a week to give me progress reports and ask my advice on various matters.

The opportunity to help Oscar was a rewarding experience. I found great satisfaction in passing some of what I've learned along.

Reach out.

What I have long known instinctively was confirmed by Dr. J. Hornik, a researcher at the University of Chicago. He found that a brief light touch on the upper arm of a person you are talking with forms a bond on a subconscious level. It is subconsciously interpreted as an expression of warmth and a friendly desire to bond.

The mentor learns more than the protégé.

Find a protégé who values your advice and experience. You'll learn a lot by giving it.

The one question you must answer.

You must be able to answer the question at the heart of both business and personal relationships. Regardless of whether you are dealing with family, friends, customers, or employees, you must have a clear and compelling answer to their unspoken question: "What's in it for me?"

What may be "in it" for some may simply be a chance to express their love for you. Others receive pleasure by demonstrating their friendship. While there's no material reward for altruism, it feels good.

Once you leave the gentle realm of love and friendship and enter the business world, the game is played by a different set of rules. People are not generally motivated by love or altruism. Though the question is rarely asked, most people want a clear understanding of what they will get in exchange for their time and money. They want to know if what you are offering will advance their careers, feed them, be entertaining, help them gain prestige, protect them, save them money—the list goes on.

The more you offer, the more you get in return.

Now that's integrity!

If you don't have integrity, you have nothing.

— HENRY KRAVIS, AMERICAN
BUSINESSMAN

I once had a funky little office in an industrial park. My landlord, a retired Realtor, was a kindly older gentleman who would sometimes stop by my office with homegrown tomatoes. He loved to chat.

One day I was having lunch with him in his office when the mail arrived. As we talked, he casually slit open envelopes and set them aside. He was talking when he opened the last envelope but stopped abruptly when he looked inside. It contained a check for $30,000.

Some months back he had referred a person who was looking to purchase beachfront property to a former colleague. He never thought about the referral again and had no knowledge of the completed transaction. The accompanying note simply said, "Thank you for the referral." He told me that the party sending the check had no obligation to do so. He read the note again and then held the check up for me to see. He said, "That, my friend, is integrity."

We have a technical problem.

Although they are essential to any enterprise, they may present a communication problem. I'm talking about technical people.

Technical brains tend to have black-and-white wiring. This is an essential attribute for anyone working with the immutable laws of numbers and data.

The black-and-white wiring of technical brain circuitry usually won't accommodate much gray abstraction. Often such brains let numbers override common sense. It's difficult for them to appreciate G. O. Ashley's observation, "Numbers are symbols for things. The number and the thing are not the same."

Of course there are exceptions to this rule, and not all technical people have this hard-wiring problem. Whether they do or not, always remember that, in their world, techies are smarter and more talented than you.

It is important to know a few rules for communicating with techies:

* Don't switch topics without making it clear that you are moving on to another subject. Techies are linear in their thinking, and they tend to bring elements from the previously discussed subject forward to the next topic.

* Avoid using analogies and similes. Technical people tend to be very literal. I once negotiated with a techie for some programming services I needed. He quoted his price to do the work, which I accepted by saying (mistakenly), "That seems more than fair." It was a bad choice of words because the next day, he called me to say he would have to raise the price. He told me he wanted the price to be fair instead of "more than fair." I explained that it was just a figure of speech, but it was too late. The mouse trap had already been sprung.

* Use simple unambiguous language. Your personal opinion on a matter is not going to count for much unless it is backed up with proof that the techie can understand and accept.

Get agreement.

A restaurateur in Chicago, after doing a little arithmetic, estimated that he was losing $600,000 per year on no-shows. People made reservations, but did not show up. He instructed the people taking reservations to not only get the parties' name and phone number, but to also get their agreement, which was simply to ask them a question: "Will you call us if you can't keep this reservation?"

Obviously, everyone would say yes, which established a subtle physiological contract. This phrase replaced the simple, "Please call us if you can't make this reservation," which was only a request, not an agreement.

Know the importance of a first impression.

Nobody counts the number of ads you run; they just remember the impression you make. —WILLIAM BERNBACH, AMERICAN
ADVERTISING EXECUTIVE

As unlikely as it may seem, research shows that a first impression is made within the first three seconds. That initial impression is confirmed or changed within the next fifteen seconds of a conversation.

There are a lot of factors you should consider in order to make a million-dollar first impression. Facial expression, posture, dress, tone of voice, and handshake are significant factors in creating that impression.

I can't resist relating one of the worst first impressions I've ever witnessed. I was running a community newspaper serving a small beach town. I had an appointment with a job applicant for a sales position. Fifteen minutes after the appointed time, the receptionist buzzed me and said, "You're nine o'clock is here." I detected a strained hysteria in her voice.

The applicant entered my office with a parrot on his shoulder. He was barefoot and had a long red beard down to his waist and was eating an apple which he was sharing with the parrot.

The first words out of my mouth were "Who put you up to this?"

He looked at me blankly and said, "What are you talking about?"

I explained, "I can't imagine you representing our newspaper to the business community." To which he responded, "Well, I've done a lot of selling."

I asked him what kind of selling had he done, and he said, "Tending bar and that's selling, man."

As you can imagine, it was a short interview.

Let it be their idea.

When discussing an idea, I have found that often it is smart to introduce elements into a conversation that suggest a solution, but I never state the solution. As such a conversation proceeds, the other party will suggest the solution—the one you had in mind all along.

At this point, you would be well served by exclaiming, "Perfect!" or "Brilliant!" and consider the deal done.

Devious? I don't know. I've been married a long time and have had a lot of experience on the receiving end.

Dial it back.

How often have you met someone you immediately didn't like?

Call it a personality conflict. Research into this "oil and water" phenomenon suggests a lot of factors are at work, most of which are beyond your control.

While you can't control a negative reaction, you might be able to soften it.

I'm well over six feet tall, and I have often noticed a reaction to my height. My guess is that subconsciously some people find me threatening.

When I meet new people, I try to lessen this reaction. I relax, smile, speak in a soft voice, and avoid prolonged eye contact for the first five minutes or so of a conversation.

Let's shake on it.

I can feel the twinkle of his eye in his handshake. —HELEN KELLER

In today's world of virtual offices, online meetings, telephone and e-mail marketing, and Internet selling, it is easy to lose sight of the importance of your handshake.

Your handshake speaks volumes about you. It can convey confidence, warmth, and honesty, or it can signal weakness, uncertainty, and disinterest. Whether positive or negative, your handshake sends a message—a message that is not lost on people.

Your handshake is a powerful business asset that can help you make a winning impression that opens doors and closes deals. Working on it is time well spent. Here are a few tips:

- ✳ *Avoid the gorilla grip:* A handshake should be firm, but not forceful. A power grip can be interpreted as aggressive. If you have a power grip, resistance to you will go up a notch or two. In some cultures, it's considered rude and aggressive.
- ✳ *Nothing wimpy:* It's amazing how many businesspeople offer weak, perfunctory handshakes. This is a major turnoff to many.
- ✳ *Look 'em in the eye:* As you extend your hand, establish eye contact and smile. Show some teeth. A warm and sincere greeting can make you an instant friend. And all things being equal, people prefer to do business with friends. Posture is also important, so stand erect when shaking someone's hand.
- ✳ *Practice makes perfect:* Much like dancing, the fine art of the handshake takes practice. Stand before a mirror and extend your hand. Check to see if you're projecting an image of confidence, warmth, and enthusiasm. Keep in mind that your handshake reflects your personality and should be a spontaneous gesture of friendly greeting that comes naturally from within.

You've been talking business with someone on the phone for several months and meet in person for the first time. To express your pleasure at finally meeting face-to-face, you want to cover his or her extended hand with your left hand briefly during the handshake. This increases the familiarity and warmth of the handshake. It's also a pleasant gesture when you are shaking hands with someone you've met previously. It simply says, "I'm very glad to see you again." Do not attempt this with someone you don't know.

What to say? No handshake is complete without a spoken greeting. You can't go wrong with, "It's a pleasure to meet you."

When departing, it's time to shake hands again. You now have the opportunity to leave a lasting impression. If you've connected and established rapport with the person, it's a good idea to gently grasp his or her right forearm with your left hand during the handshake, and restate your pleasure at having met the person. This two-handed shake signals a desire to, in a figurative sense, hold on to your new friend.

Make the gatekeeper your friend.

If you are trying to reach an important client or potential business partner, befriend the gatekeeper.

If the person I need to speak with is not in, I take a moment to learn the gatekeeper's name. I ask how long he or she has been with the company. Sometimes I get more information than I bargained for, such as, "I worked in this industry for 15 years. After my husband was injured, I was fortunate to get a job here."

When you next call back, your chances of getting through are greatly improved. After all, now the gatekeeper knows you.

Ask for a replay.

Whenever you instruct people to do something, have them repeat it back to you.

While this may seem demeaning, if you handle it with a little charm, you will pull it off. I always start by saying, "To make sure I didn't leave anything out, could you repeat that back to me?" It's surprising how often this little exercise reveals misunderstood directions.

Are you having fun yet?

There've been times when I've driven to work with great excitement and anticipation because I was looking forward to having fun. Business should be fun and exciting. In the end, it really is a form of playing.

The people working with you should also be having fun because fun promotes creativity, and creativity leads to success.

4 | STRICTLY SELLING

Everyone lives by selling something.

—ROBERT LOUIS STEVENSON

IF YOU ARE in business, you are in sales.

Entrepreneurs and small business owners often focus exclusively on what they believe are the essentials. Well-thought-out business and marketing plans are created. Product development and distribution strategies are conceived. Projections are made. And when the work is done, a blueprint for a business machine has been built. However, often not much thought has been given to the power source needed to run it.

Few people will disagree with the old adage, "Nothing happens until a sale is made." Still, this elementary truth is not always the first consideration in building a business.

The sales department is often underappreciated and overlooked despite the obvious relationship between sales and success. It seems to be forgotten that sales keep the lights on, pay the rent, and make payroll.

Businesses don't make money on what they produce; they make money on what they sell. A company with a mediocre product but a first-rate sales team will outsell a company with an excellent product and a mediocre sales team.

Many otherwise savvy businesspeople have a bad opinion of sales-people and look at sales as a "necessary evil." Selling is much more complicated and takes more skill than many imagine.

Selling requires prospecting, pitching, negotiating, closing, and more. It's both art and science and demands an understanding of the dynamics of the human mind and how to influence the forces that inform decision making.

You will be well served to learn more about selling because not only is it key to your success, but it is the primary means by which your company puts on a human face and meets the outside world.

Because that's where the money is.

When Willie Sutton, the infamous bank robber of the 1930s, was asked why he robbed banks, he replied, "Because that's where the money is."

Customers who have already purchased from you are more responsive than any other group to buy from you again. That's where their money is!

Make them "preferred customers." Come back to them with special deals, and let them be the first to know about new products or services you offer. Many companies offer a prerelease special discounted price right before a product goes on the market. When the product is launched, they already have orders.

Know your buyer.

The first step in exceeding your customer's expectations is to know those expectations. —ROY H. WILLIAMS, BUSINESS AUTHOR AND MARKETING CONSULTANT

"Know your buyer" is one of the most common bits of entrepreneurial advice. You'll hear it often, and usually it means knowing the demographic and psychographic makeup of your target market.

This information is frequently presented in reports, which compile data on age, gender, buying habits, and more, and is essential to effective marketing.

I decided I wanted to look beyond the cold, hard data. I wanted to meet my buyers in person and learn firsthand who they were. Here's how I did it. I called and told them that I had a gift for them and that I would like to stop by to deliver it in person. I quickly added that I had nothing to sell them.

I told them that I would like to ask a few questions about their experience with my product. I also let them know that the meeting should not take more than 10 minutes. Over half accepted my offer to visit them.

Politicians call these face-to-face meetings with their voters "pressing the flesh." They do it to garner support for their political campaigns.

Since the businesspeople I was planning to visit had already voted for me by buying my product, my purpose for "pressing the flesh" was to learn firsthand who they really were.

I started visiting only those within 50 miles of my office. When traveling out of town, I would visit customers in whatever city I was in. Within a year, I had visited nearly 100 customers.

I saw their offices, photos of their kids, and award plaques on their walls. I learned about their products or service and got their feedback on their experiences with my product. I got some good ideas on ways to improve my product.

These visits gave me a far more detailed picture of my buyer than I could ever have gotten from a report or by trying to talk to them at a chaotic trade show.

From my face-to-face meetings, I formed a mental picture that was a composite of my buyers. It has served me well. I use it when I'm developing a product or creating a marketing campaign.

Here's a "magic" formula for selling.

What's the magic selling formula that TV hucksters use to convince millions of people to pull out a credit card, call an 800 number and place an order for a product they don't need? The answer may surprise you.

No matter how silly and shifty these TV pitches are, when you scrape away the hucksterism, you see that they follow a legitimate and proven sales formula that includes creating excitement and curiosity, identifying a problem, offering a solution, reciting the benefits of ownership, establishing credibility, adding value, up-selling, and ending it all with a strong call to action.

Here's how it works.

Without exception these TV pitches are delivered by people who are wildly enthusiastic and breathlessly excited about the product they are hawking. Excitement, apparently even phony over-the-top excitement, grabs buyers' attention and arouses curiosity.

They then state a problem, "The problem with blankets is that they always slip off." The fact that people really don't have much trouble managing a blanket is immaterial. The need for their product, no matter if the need is nonexistent, is presented with great conviction.

A lengthy, fast-moving, and repetitious recital of the benefits of ownership, complete with product demonstrations, is delivered. "You will slice a tomato perfectly every time with one simple motion, and cleanup is a snap!" "You'll save time and have perfectly uniform slices for salads and sandwiches!" they add.

A studio audience paid to ooh and ah and applaud wildly in response to the product demonstrations is often used to establish credibility. Short customer testimonials are sometimes filmed and interspersed throughout the pitch for the same purpose. Statements like, "If you have a car, boat, or RV, you'd be crazy not to own one of these!" are typical.

But wait, there's more! "Act now and we'll include a second one free of charge. All you pay is shipping and handling." This offer to double the order appears to be adding value for the buyer, but in reality it's an up-sell. The shipping and handling charges more than cover the total cost of adding another unit and generate additional profit.

The seller creates a sense of urgency: "You must act now to get this special offer." "Have your credit card ready and call within the next 10 minutes, and we'll include Jill's recipes at absolutely no extra cost to you." Some even show a ticking clock counting down the time left to buy.

There's a lesson to be learned here. While the products are cheesy and the pitchmen are clownish, sales and marketing fundamentals are being closely followed.

Creating excitement and curiosity, identifying a problem, offering a solution, reciting the benefits of ownership, establishing credibility, adding value, up-selling, and ending it all with a strong call to action will close sales for nearly anyone.

Sell by the numbers.

Look at any popular news website or magazine, and you'll see headlines that pique reader interest with numbers of things. For example: "Five Foods You Should Avoid," "Seven Ways to Tell if He's Cheating on You," "Nine Ways to Lose Fifteen Pounds This Summer," or "Seven Hot Vacations Spots."

I think the popularity of presenting things this way comes from the fact that specific numbers promise nuggets of interesting information that are easy to read and understand.

Don't answer a question with a question.

Contrary to conventional sales training wisdom, it is not a good idea to answer a question with a question. While your question may be a simple request for information, it can be perceived by the prospect as evasive and manipulative. For example, if your buyer asks, "When can you ship?" do not respond, "When do you need it?" This strategy can diminish your credibility. Why not simply tell him or her your estimated shipping time. If that's not soon enough, then learn the desired delivery date and do your best to make it happen.

Eight reasons you might be losing sales.

1. *Your sales pitch is boring.* Do customers cut you off in midsentence or jump in when you pause for breath? Chances are you're boring them. Paint a vivid picture and put them in it; use an example or interesting case history to illustrate your point. Whip out some visuals to show them how much money they will save.

2. *You insult their intelligence.* "Mr. Jones, would you like to save money on your long-distance phone bill?" Polling prospects with lame questions in an attempt to get them to say yes is manipulative and insulting. Instead, ask open-ended questions to elicit their needs. Treat them with respect by tailoring your questions to their company, industry, and circumstances.

3. *You are uninformed.* Take time to visit the website of your prospect's company. Check out its competition, industry association, and trade journals. Remember: the more you learn, the more you earn. If you do not understand what your prospects do and what issues they face, how can you expect to determine how your product or service can best help them?

4. *You are talking to the wrong person.* Oops! Once again, you have not done your homework, and you end up pitching someone who has no decision-making authority. This hurts because it's usually hard to get a second bite of the apple.

5. *You do not listen.* Pay attention to what your customers are saying and how they are saying it, including their nonverbal communication. Effective listening provides you with most of the answers to your qualifying questions without even asking them. You will learn about your customers' needs, what their hot buttons are, and how to convince them you can satisfy their needs. Simply put: when your customer talks, you sell; when you talk, you lose.

6. *You do not understand their needs.* In the world of sales, one size rarely fits all. Find out your prospects' special needs and concerns, and show how your product or service can help. Again: listen, and they will tell you.

7. *Buyers do not like you.* You have heard it a million times: people buy from people they like. If your prospect doesn't like you, he's not going to spend time getting to know your product or service. Investing some time in your rapport-building skills will pay big dividends.

8. *They do not know you and have never heard of your company.* All things being equal, who do you think your prospect is going to buy from? The company she has known for years, or you, the new kid on the block? Allay her fears by providing her with current customer lists (including contact names and numbers for some of your accounts), testimonial letters on your customers' letterhead, documented case histories, and press coverage. A referral from someone she knows and respects will swing doors wide open.

It's the little things that make a difference in sales. Pay attention to these eight factors and make more sales.

Do you need props?

There are two schools of thought on the best way to make a presentation. One school says that slides, flip cards, brochures, product samples, and demonstrations are the best ways to interest investors and potential customers in your enterprise. The other school advises ditching the props and going into a meeting "naked."

The theory is that going "propless" focuses the attention on you and what you are saying rather than requiring the other party to sit through a pitch.

I think the best way to go is a blend of these two approaches, thus keeping the props to a minimum and promoting a "nonsalesy" business conversation.

Learn Telephone 101.

If you prospect or sell by telephone, don't wing it. Save your sanity and invest in professional training.

I try to take all sales and prospecting calls. As publisher of a sales and business growth newsletter, it's part of my job. I want to analyze the pitches and learn from them. Beyond the selling insights I sometimes gain, there is always the chance that the salesperson calling is offering something I want or need. I take the call and listen.

Many of these calls are painfully amateurish or high-pressure pitches. It's little wonder buyers view salespeople as unwelcome intruders, hide behind their voice mail, and don't return calls.

Buyer disdain and mistrust are also the reasons that you encounter skepticism, suspicion, impatience, and disinterest.

Because buyers are besieged with annoying calls, the deck is stacked against you. However, there are ways you can give yourself an advantage and successfully engage buyers.

The more direct you are the better. Example: "Hi, Bob, this is Jane Smith with Acme Solutions. The reason I'm calling you this morning is to find out if we can (name the benefit) for you. I won't waste your time. We can either help you, or we can't. It will take us just a few minutes to find out."

Note that the phrase "I won't waste your time" is music to the prospect's ears. This opening can be adapted to almost any product or service you are selling.

This very basic advice is a start, but if you are going to contact prospects by phone, you owe it to yourself to make the best use of your time. Call on an expert for a bit of training before you start.

Reflect on your calls.

Some people who struggle with telephone communications look in a mirror when they're on the phone so that they can see themselves when they are talking. The theory is that body language, posture, and facial expressions all come through over the phone.

Master the art of the up-sell.

Today on the way to the office I stopped for my morning fix at the local coffee shop. No hazelnut harvest latte for me. Just a plain cup of joe, thank you. When I placed my order, the barista smiled and said, "Would you like a low-fat poppy seed muffin with that? They're still warm. Just took 'em out of the oven."

I was surprised to hear myself saying, "Sure."

The up-sell is an important way to increase the revenues of your business. A few summers ago, I read an ad offering an excellent price on a rototiller. I called the company and told the sales representative what I wanted. He asked what type of soil I would be working. I told him it was a mixture of loam and clay. He asked how difficult it would be to turn the soil with a spade, and I let him know that it would be fairly difficult because the soil was compact and hard.

He suggested that I get a model with twice the horse power for just a few hundred dollars more with an extended warranty and free shipping. He gave me a compelling reason to accept the up-sell, so I accepted.

Another perhaps less obvious example of the up-sell is the "impulse items" you'll find at any supermarket checkout. These include candy, chewing gum, salty snacks, and gossip rags. As you're standing in line, they let these items up-sell themselves.

This dog won't hunt.

When you're interviewing a candidate for a sales position, always ask, "How much money did you make last year?" If the candidate is shy about talking about the previous year's earnings, take a pass. If the applicant is shy about talking money with you, odds are he or she will be uncomfortable talking about money with a prospect.

The ideal candidate will introduce the subject and ask, "How much can I make?" within the first 20 or 30 minutes of an interview.

If a salesperson is the least hesitant at talking money, she or he is probably not the hungry carnivore you need. This dog won't hunt.

Don't ask what their budget is; tell them what it is.

I was looking to buy a used truck for my small ranch. I didn't need anything fancy, just something functional for hauling firewood, fertilizer, and feed.

I drove past a used car lot and saw an old Ford truck which looked like a perfect candidate for the job. I stopped and was looking the truck over when a salesman approached. I asked him the price of the truck. He responded by asking, "How much do you want to pay?" Not wanting to play the salesman's games, I thanked him and quickly left.

Similarly, one of the lamest questions I'm asked by vendors while inquiring about their service is, "What's your budget for this?"

My response is always, "I won't be able to formulate a budget until I know what your charges are." I sometimes add, "How will knowing my budget help you determine your price?"

It is always better to tell potential clients their cost early on in a business conversation. This establishes your honesty. You'll quickly learn whether it's in their budget or not.

Don't call me. I'll call you.

I sympathize with anyone trying to make a living by cold-calling prospects. It's a tough hustle, and only a few succeed at it.

Because of the unprofessional telephone sales tactics of some, the well has been poisoned for all. Yet, despite the difficulty of selling on the phone, the calls keep coming in.

Anyone in business is forced to take defensive measures against unwanted phone solicitations.

While you may refuse to accept unsolicited sales calls, never ask anyone to lie for you, as in, "Tell him I'm not in." This is bad business form and shows weak leadership.

When a salesperson calls, have whoever is taking the call instruct the caller to send an e-mail. Have the screener ask the caller to put STAR in the subject line of the e-mail so you will know the person has called and you won't summarily delete the e-mail. This makes the rejection easier for the caller and, who knows, you may have an interest in what is being sold or proposed. Although unlikely, the call could also be about a wonderful business opportunity.

Of course, the most effective junkyard dog of a gatekeeper is voice mail. I worked with one CEO whose voice mail message concludes with, "If I don't know you or the reason you're calling, please don't expect a return call."

There will be times when you will be the one making the cold call. You may be calling to discuss an affiliate arrangement, check out a reference, or other business not related to selling. While you won't be selling anything, you will be screened as if you were. Your call will be much more likely to be put through if you give your company and your name and title and state the reason for your call and add, "Please tell her that this is not a sales call."

Gain your buyer's trust.

Use confidence enhancers to let potential buyers know that yours is a company they can trust.

Usually the first thing customers see is the graphic look of your company. Opinions are formed in seconds. So your graphic look should convey your professionalism. Have a professionally designed and well-executed graphic look for your brochures, stationery, business cards, letterhead, and website. This immediately builds your company's credibility.

Remember that quality writing is essential. The written word is the voice of your company. Keep it intelligent, friendly, and informative. In the words of my writer friend, Herb Lockwood, "The human eye is repelled by a sea of type." Never be afraid to use plenty of white space.

Testimonials are another powerful tool in gaining trust. They should include the name and city of the person giving the testimony. Testimonials given by a company executive should include the name of the company as well as the name and title of the person giving the testimonial.

Case histories build confidence with your prospective customers. Make them interesting and demonstrate how a benefit was gained or a problem solved. Include numbers in case histories. Make them engaging by including before and after stories. Keep them brief. A short paragraph or two for each case history will do.

Mentioning your business affiliations and current clients is another way to build trust. If you are doing business with a nationally known company, let buyers know.

If you accept orders online, all of the following elements should appear on your order page:

* Logos of the credit cards that you accept along with a web security logo.
* If you use a shipping company, its logo should also appear.
* Include a restatement of your guarantee, your phone number, and company logo. I even include my company's street address.

The reason for all this is that a surprisingly high number of buyers abandon the order page. They will go all the way to the order page and then have second thoughts and not buy. When this happens, it is usually not because they no longer want the product. They bail out because of a lack of confidence in the company.

You don't need a company mission statement. No one is interested. Few people read these often self-aggrandizing essays. And those who do read them are not influenced to buy a product.

Offer a strong guarantee, and back it up. No weasel words. An iron-clad guarantee makes a strong statement about your company and the quality and value of its product or service. Live up to your guarantee.

Your full company contact information including street address and phone numbers should be included. If you are offering a special deal such as free shipping, highlight it. State your prices, shipping details, and the methods of payment you accept.

One size does not fit all.

If you are delivering the same basic pitch over and over, you are undoubtedly losing sales. Take a lesson from the U.S. Marines and "improvise, adapt, and overcome." This requires listening to and reading your prospect. You must always be thinking on your feet and adapting your pitch in real time to what you are hearing from your buyer. It's no easy feat, but those who master this skill close far more sales than those who don't.

Everybody loves to buy, but nobody likes to be sold.

Sales training and motivational legend, Jeffrey Gitomer, has made the above statement famous. It applies not only to selling, but to business in general. If you give people a compelling reason to do business with you, they almost always will. However, it seems to be part of human DNA that if you try to pressure or corner them, they resist you mightily.

It's especially important that everyone selling for your company be aware of this simple but powerful truth.

How can they sell it for that?

Retailers use the term *loss leader* to describe an item that is sold at or below cost. The idea, of course, is to attract bargain hunters with the lowered price who will then make other purchases while they're at the store.

Some years back, I became friends with the co-owner of a sports clothing manufacturer and distributor. He was responsible for the company's sales and marketing. We occasionally had lunch together. Even though these were not business lunches, our conversations would often turn to marketing.

Each year, the company had a parking lot sale to liquidate excess inventory. A wide array of sports apparel was offered at bargain prices. The parking lot sales, held on weekends, were not nearly as well attended as my buddy would like. Despite a decent ad budget, he wasn't generating the turnout he needed. Part of his problem was that his facility was located off the main road in an industrial park, and he couldn't rely on drive-by traffic.

One day at lunch he asked me, "How can I get more people out to these sales?"

I couldn't think of anything he hadn't already tried, but I promised to give it some thought.

That weekend, I drove past a volunteer fire department's pancake breakfast. The parking lot was jammed, and there were cars waiting to get in.

The following week I lunched with my pal again. "Why don't you have a pancake breakfast at your parking lot sale?" I asked. He laughed at the idea, but I could see that the wheels were turning.

He asked if I really thought that would generate a crowd. I said, "It might if the price of the pancakes is one dollar."

He smiled and said, "Oh, a loss leader. I guess I'll have to give this some thought."

A couple of days later he called to tell me it was a go. The annual sale was about six weeks away, which gave him enough time to make the arrangements for the event. He did his usual advertising. The first day of the event, he posted directional signs with arrows emblazoned with "Pancake Breakfast $1."

On Saturday the event drew a much bigger crowd than usual. But on Sunday he got an incredible response. The place was a mob scene. Crowds of people showed up. Some had learned of the bargain prices from people who had shopped there on Saturday. Others came for the one-dollar pancakes and stayed to shop. The cash register kept ringing.

While the company lost money on the one-dollar pancakes, it more than quadrupled the previous year's sales.

Now that's salesmanship!

Salesmanship is limitless. Our very living is selling. We are all salespeople. —James Cash Penney

A friend who owns a printing company had set aside an afternoon to interview applicants for a sales opening with his firm.

The last applicant of the day showed up and, after a preliminary chat, opened his laptop and began a slide show. The first slide indicated that the presentation was made especially for the owner of the printing company. It proceeded with charts that showed the growth of the applicant's sales for the past three years. Next came quotes in enlarged type taken from his references. He then went on with quotes from testimonials his buyers had given him. He also showed a slide with the logos of the companies that had bought from him.

He followed that with a picture of himself and his family and one taken of him with the Little League team he coached. He concluded with a slide with a headline that read "Five Reasons You Should Hire Me."

The applicant had cleverly turned the job interview into a sales presentation to demonstrate his sales abilities. At the end of the five-minute presentation my friend had just one question, "When can you start?"

Learn to listen.

When people talk, listen completely. Most people never listen.
— ERNEST HEMINGWAY

Develop your listening skills. Good listeners close far more sales than people without good listening skills. Period.

I recently received a call from a salesperson with an annoying rapid-fire staccato delivery. He didn't even allow me to answer his questions before plunging forward and talking over me. Within a few minutes I was developing a headache and had completely tuned this guy out. When he had finally finished his pitch, I jokingly asked, "Could you repeat that?" He didn't respond. I then offered to send him a link to information that would help him improve his phone skills. He declined my offer and hung up.

Obviously Mr. Rapid Fire never heard of the 80-20 rule which states that the prospect should do 80 percent of the talking and that the salesperson should do 20 percent. Frankly, I think the rule, while a good guideline, is a bit difficult to adhere to especially on a first call. However, if you slow down and ask intelligent questions that get the prospect talking, you'll close a lot more sales. Shoot for a 70-30 split, and you'll be in excellent shape.

Get emotional.

When you are presenting your product or service, do not attempt to appeal strictly to the buyers' rational mind with a list of perfectly logical reasons to buy. Instead, fire their imaginations and appeal to their emotions. Stress the benefits and rewards of owning your product or using your services. Use colorfully worded illustrations that stress benefits.

Sprinkle in some brief case histories. Be likable. Have some fun. Smile. Above all, let the customer do most of the talking. Take the pressure to buy out of the experience, and the successful close will come naturally.

What do business buyers want?

What does that corporate buyer sitting behind that big mahogany desk really want from you? It's surprisingly simple: to make their jobs easier, to make them look good to management, to gain respect and prestige, to advance their careers, to be appreciated, to save time, to have some fun and excitement, and to minimize their personal risk.

Target high-value opportunities.

Make a list of the top 10 companies with which you would like to do business. Once you've identified them, write what I'll call an "opportunity acquisition plan." Include in your plan the steps you'll need to take to reach your goal. The elements of your plan should include detailed research on each company, its history, information on the principals, and the identification of decision makers. Learn about its industry.

Find someone you know who knows people in the targeted company and whose referral may open doors.

When you do contact the target organization, have something compelling to say that you know will be of interest to the person you're talking to.

Look sharp.

This advice bears repeating: the old cliché about dressing for success still holds true.

Your clothes and personal grooming speak volumes about you to buyers, team members, and investors. If you are looking good, you are undoubtedly feeling good, and you will be more confident.

Take a critical look at your appearance, keeping in mind that shoes are one of the first things noticed. Your working wardrobe should be of high quality and made up entirely of the following materials: cotton, wool, silk, linen, and leather. That's it.

There are several good books on sharp dressing and good grooming. John T. Molloy's *New Dress for Success* is an update of the classic.

Use a built-in up-sell.

Daniel Herbert, a subscriber to my newsletter, tells the story of a popular bakery in his hometown that makes excellent sheet cakes. When a customer picks up a cake, it's in the aluminum baking pan in which it was baked.

Customers pay a modest deposit on the pan which is refunded when the pan is returned. At the time of purchase customers are told that they may keep the pan or return it for their refund. The bakery purchases the pans in bulk at a wholesale price which is half the price of the deposit.

Many people opt not to return the pan because the deposit is about the retail price of the pan.

Now the question arises: does this little bakery sell cakes or cake pans? It turns out that it's selling both. Dan isn't sure if there's a name for this up-sell concept but wonders what other businesses could use it to add a few more dollars to their bottom line.

Gimmicks work . . . sometimes.

You gotta have a gimmick. — Stephen Sondheim

Salespeople can get a little crazy trying to get the attention of a potential buyer.

There is the story of the salesman who bought a pair of shoes and sent just one to a prospect he had not been able to reach. He attached this note: "Now that I have one foot in the door . . ."

As the story goes, the prospect was amused and took his next call.

The salesman who sent a three-minute egg-timer and a note, which read "Set this when you take my call, and I'll be done before the bell goes off," deserves a special mention.

One person wrote a check for the amount his prospective business affiliate would gain through a joint business relationship. He put, "Next year's increased income" in the memo section, and then wrote VOID across the check, and sent it with a note that read, "Your next one can be ready to cash."

One person I know routinely sends a lottery ticket to someone who is hard to reach. "You'll have a much greater chance for making money if you take a moment to talk with me."

File this one under chutzpah. This isn't something I would ever advise, but it illustrates the lengths some salespeople will go to in order to get a prospect's attention. A very aggressive salesman I know relates this story. He was having a difficult time getting through to a promising prospect. He had called the buyer's office countless times but could never get past the gatekeeper who always asked, "May I tell him what this is about?" After a few minutes on hold she would return to tell him the prospect was not available.

One afternoon he called the prospect's office and, when asked what his call was about, he exclaimed, "It's about my wife!" Within a few minutes the annoyed prospect was on the line.

"Why are you calling me about your wife?"

The salesman replied, "I had a long talk with her last night, and she told me she would leave me if I didn't start making more sales."

There was a long silence before the prospect started laughing. He agreed to a brief meeting with the salesman.

I confess I have used a gimmick or two in the past. I once had my graphics department create an article about the CEO of a company which copied the graphic style of a *Wall Street Journal* article.

It was dated a month into the future. The headline read, "Bob Smith Named Entrepreneur of the Year." The faux story, which had my byline, went on to explain how his company increased its bottom line by a fantastic amount. The quote, which was attributed to him, mentioned our company and how we were one of the key elements of his success. The story concluded with how sharply his company's stock prices had risen.

When I next called him, we both had a good laugh. Whether or not the fake article had anything to do with it or not, we ended up doing business together.

One of the funnier and most attention-grabbing gimmicks I've heard of is the salesperson who sent a ransom note to a prospect. The note was crafted from words clipped from various publications which were pasted on a sheet of paper to read, "We are holding thousands of your customers. If you ever want to see them again, talk with Bob Smith within forty-eight hours. He is the only person who can help you save them. Signed: A friend."

Whether he ultimately closed the sale or not, I'm certain he got the buyer's attention.

5 MARKETING ISN'T ROCKET SCIENCE ... IT'S HARDER!

WHILE THEY ARE kissing cousins and sometimes overlap, sales and marketing are not the same.

Marketing covers advertising, promotion, market research, public relations, and, to some degree, sales. In the simplest terms, it is the process of identifying and locating buyers and introducing and promoting products and services to them.

Despite its importance, surprisingly many entrepreneurs don't know much about marketing. While they understand the basic concepts, to them it's a mundane subject. However, it is one of the most mysterious and demanding aspects of business.

It requires knowledge of marketing technologies, a keen understanding of what motivates buyers and how to press their hot buttons, a masterful command of language, the ability to create and deliver compelling and memorable messages, and analytical thinking.

Marketing is not a do-it-yourself job. The talent and creativity needed to do it well are rare. There are no easy-to-follow formulas. Marketing is no place for amateurs.

Marketing strategies have changed radically in recent years. Channels that were undreamed of five years ago, such as mobile and social media marketing, are now taken for granted. New channels are continually emerging. With the many new ways to reach them, so many messages are bombarding consumers that it is now more difficult than ever to get your product noticed, so marketers have learned to be creative.

Unless you are a marketing professional, you will need help. Marketing agencies and professional marketing consultants will be able to help you reach your business goals quicker and, in the end, a lot more cheaply than you can if you do it yourself. Expect sticker shock. First-rate marketing does not come cheap. Enterprises without the budget and a strong marketing mindset are at a very real disadvantage in today's supercompetitive business world.

This chapter does not introduce you to the new "gee whiz" marketing. It contains old-school advice on some of the marketing fundamentals that will never change regardless of how much technology does.

Making a marketing reality check.

Business has only two functions—marketing and innovation.

—MILAN KUNDERA, CZECH NOVELIST

It's remarkable how many people think that, by starting a business, they have somehow become marketing experts.

The basic concepts are simple and easy to understand, but, like many things, the devil is in the details. The old adage about poker comes to mind: It takes a minute to learn and a lifetime to master.

While marketing doesn't take a lifetime to master, unless you have a few years of successful marketing experience, you don't know much about marketing.

I suspect that business loses millions, perhaps billions, each year both from the cost of paying for marketing that doesn't work and sales lost by amateurish marketing.

Hire or retain a marketing professional to manage this all-important function. A marketing pro will accelerate your business growth and generate revenue for you far in excess of the cost.

Of course, you will have questions. You will want to see plans, budgets, and projections, and you will want to be kept informed, but resist the urge to second-guess or meddle in the details.

The line is long because the line is long.

A few blocks from my former office, in a small resort town, was an immensely popular cafe. The little cafe was opened for breakfast and lunch only. The food was good, albeit pricey.

On weekdays, there always seemed to be a line of a dozen people or so waiting to get in. Weekends the line was often half a block long.

When the landlord approached the owner and offered to expand the size of the place, she turned him down. "Those people standing in front of my place waiting to get in are the best advertising I could ever hope to buy," she told him.

The fact that the town had a lot of tourists on vacation, with the time to wait, undoubtedly contributed to the long line.

The owner understood and exploited the customer's rationale that it's unlikely that such a large group could be wrong, and if people were willing to wait in line to eat, the food must really be good.

It seems to be a hardwired human attribute. Crowds draw crowds. The line is long because the line is long.

There can be too much information.

Information is not knowledge. —ALBERT EINSTEIN

I started reading a company's brochure recently, but I didn't make it to page 4. The company's 24-page brochure tried to include every possible detail. It started with the histories of their industry and their company. It continued with a long discourse on how its products were manufactured. It was tightly packed with type with only a few graphic elements and no photographs. I am very sure no one, with the exception of those who created it, ever read it from cover to cover. Too much nonsalient information presented in a boring format is a sure sign that amateur marketers are at work. The day you receive a call from a prospective buyer who says, "I am considering buying your product but I need to know more about the history of your industry," is the same day you'll see unicorns frolicking in the parking lot.

The question should not be, "What did we leave out?" but, "What can we leave out?"

An effective brochure, whether printed or online, should be created with one goal in mind, which is making the sale. Buyers are distracted and bored by superfluous information. It is extremely naïve to think that the purpose of a brochure is to give the buyer an education about any subject beyond your product or service.

Buyers are attracted by an attention-grabbing headline. Sometimes a subhead is effective when it's stating your guarantee or listing of a few additional benefits. The primary headline should embody the main benefit of ownership. Your clever headline should be followed by a list of clearly stated benefits. Case histories and testimonials with the names and head shots of those making them might also be a good idea. Use well-executed graphics and leave plenty of white space.

Most important, have a strong call to action. Tell your prospects what to do next, and make it easy for them to do it.

Tell them three times.

Repetition makes reputation and reputation makes customers.
— Elizabeth Arden

Effective advertising and prospecting letters rely on repetition. The use of repetition to get an idea across may be why we watch the same commercial on TV over and over.

I have a close friend who is a brilliant copywriter. He has worked for many national advertisers. His clients keep coming back for more. He tells me that his secret lies in repetition. I can understand the rationale for repeating an ad many times on TV, but in a prospecting letter? Sounds a bit strange, but he assures me that it works.

Here's his formula, which he may have adapted from Aristotle's advice on making speeches: First he gets buyers' interest with an attention-grabbing headline which states or suggests a benefit. In a smaller sub-headline he tells them what he's going to tell them. In the body of the copy he tells them. Then he closes by telling them what he has told them.

Of course, it takes real copywriting talent to pull this off in a way that flows and doesn't sound repetitious, despite the fact that it is repetitious.

Walk back in history.

When business goes flat, I try to remember a time when business was booming. I re-create everything that was happening at that time in my mind. I'll even find mailings that we sent out when times were better, and I'll send one out again. The purpose of all this is not to try to re-create the past, but to capture the spirit of a time in the company's history when things were booming. This exercise gives me ideas for change.

They won't call back.

I once served as a full-time consultant to a small software company. I met weekly with its executive team—every Monday morning at 7 a.m. Coffee and muffins were always in the conference room, and we jokingly referred to this weekly meeting as the "Monday Morning Muffin Meeting."

I came to the meeting one week at the appointed time and noticed that all the phone lines were lit up, but not being answered. I said to the company owner, "Shouldn't we be answering these phones?" I did not consider that 7 a.m. on the West Coast is 10 a.m. on the East Coast. The customer service personnel who answered the phones were instructed to start work at 9 a.m., which is noon in New York City.

I said again, "I really think we should be answering these phones." The head of the technical team, who had developed the product said, "Don't worry about it; if they want it, they will call back."

The customer service manager, who was a self-described Minnesota farm girl, knew the value of harvesting when you can. She said, "Michael's right," and excused herself from the meeting, rounded up some people from her customer service team and the shipping department and gave them all order intake forms. Then she had them start taking incoming calls.

Both the development team manager and the CEO were annoyed at the meeting disruption. At the end of the meeting, the CEO called me aside and informed me that he did not appreciate my telling his employees what to do. Without arguing, I told him I understood.

When I returned to my office, there was a message for me to call him. I suspected that the relationship would be terminated. When I called him back, I was pleasantly surprised when he apologized for chastising me and told me the sales in that two-hour period exceeded $10,000.

Connect creatively.

Gifts seduce both men and Gods. — OVID

I was working with a barter broker in New York who suddenly stopped returning my phone calls. We were working on a very sweet deal for my company, and I didn't want to lose it. I left several voice messages and sent a number of e-mail messages. Nothing.

Determined to get her attention, I sent her an expensive little plush teddy bear with a note that read, "Don't worry, I don't bite. We just need to talk."

A few days later, she called me. She was gushing, "Oh, I just love it. What a sweet gift! Thank you, thank you, and thank you!"

She apologized profusely for not getting back with me and offered a laundry list of reasons why she hadn't.

She promised me that she would go to work and get the deal closed. It was closed within a week. Thank you, Teddy.

Offer a platinum version of your product or service.

You can justify a higher price and up-sell to a significant number of customers, but you cannot sell low-cost or no-cost packaging at a higher price. Many people want quality and added value and are willing to pay a higher price to get it.

Service justifies price.

I drive an older luxury car. Its glory days are long behind it, but I still like it. For many years I had the car serviced at an independent garage. When the garage owner retired and closed his shop, I decided to try the local dealership.

I arrived at the dealership at the appointed time and was greeted by a well-dressed woman who said, "Good morning! My name is Jan, I'm your service concierge. Your service representative is John Nelson. Have a seat in his office, and he'll be right with you. May I bring you a cup of coffee?"

John entered his office a few minutes later and, after a few questions about the service I needed, had me sign the work order and directed me to the car rental desk to get a loaner. I was surprised to see that the car rental desk in the dealership lobby was run by a national company. I was informed that the loaner was free. After filling out the paperwork, I was led to a new car and given the keys. The entire process was quick and painless. Within about a half hour I was tooling down the road to my office.

I went back that afternoon, returned the loaner, and paid for the service. I was delighted to see that my car had been washed and that the interior had been vacuumed. There was a handwritten note on the driver's seat on the back of Jan's business card which read, "Thanks for the opportunity to be of service. We hope to see you again."

The amount charged was about 25 percent more than I was used to paying, but the added service justified the higher price.

When you consider that auto dealers make far more money servicing the vehicles they sell than they do in selling them, you understand the wisdom in giving the high-level service I received. And, yes, I now use them exclusively.

Prime the pump.

An interesting illustration of how buyers are followers was taught to me by, of all people, the woman who runs a drive-through coffee kiosk. Her tip jar was usually filled with a lot of dollar bills. She revealed to me that she always begins her day by putting two one-dollar bills in her glass tip jar. The presence of the dollar bills in the tip jar tells customers not only to tip, but the appropriate amount. She told me that on the days she would forget to prime the pump, her tip jar would fill much slower.

An idea is born.

Kristy Aurand, a subscriber to my newsletter, tells this story, which illustrates that you never know when an event will trigger a brilliant marketing idea.

> I sold advertising for a minor league baseball team in my hometown. It wasn't an easy sell so our sales team was trained to leave no stone unturned in finding potential sponsors.
>
> During my annual visit to my OB/GYN doctor the conversation turned to our minor league baseball team's fortunes. I learned my doctor was a season ticket holder, and I naturally started talking about the sponsorship opportunities at the stadium. As we talked, we came up with a never-before-seen promotion: "Labor Day at the Ballpark," the promotion would focus not on the American workforce, but on pregnant women. She signed a $4,000 sponsorship deal a week later. This amusing promotion got good publicity and was a big success. The retelling of this story helped me land my current job.

The market is interested in benefits, not features.

Sell benefits, not features. Even though an army of marketing experts has been giving this advice for years, it has never gained traction.

Many of the websites I visit are little more than product specification sheets. This would be okay if they were selling scientific testing equipment or storage tanks. But many of these sites are trying to sell business and consumer products with little more than a list of features.

No one is really interested in the fact that your product has a certain feature. People want to know how that feature benefits them. Does it save time or money? Is it fun or entertaining? Does it give them status? Does it simplify or improve their lives? Sell them benefits of ownership, not product features.

For example, features of a power mower may be a four-stroke engine, a wider cutting area, and an oversized catch bag. Does this mean longer engine life, less time to spend mowing, and fewer times to empty the catch bag? Say so!

Buyers are bored by features and excited by benefits. In sales and marketing the buyer's emotions come first. So start selling those benefits.

You have nothing to lose.

Years ago my father and I were driving across the Mojave Desert. We passed a big billboard announcing, "Cold drinks, Groceries, and Gasoline one mile ahead." In the smaller print it read, "See our Desert Reptile Garden." After gassing up, we were sipping sodas in the shade of a salt cypress tree when we were approached by the Reptile Garden's tour guide. He invited us to take the tour for just 75 cents each. (Remember, this was a long time ago.) I wanted to do it, but my father wasn't too enthused. I remember him saying that we had to get back on the road.

The tour operator then made a compelling proposition.

"I'll tell you what. Don't pay me anything now. If you don't enjoy the tour, you owe me nothing."

My dad accepted, and the tour was entertaining and educational. After the tour, my dad happily paid the admission price. I learned a lot about desert reptiles that day and got a lesson on guarantees as well.

A consultant I know offers to evaluate a company's online marketing materials by using a proposition that's hard to refuse. He is an expert in his field, and consequently his hourly rate is high. He targets small businesses and start-ups so he needs a guarantee that assures clients of the value of his service. It goes like this: His review of the online marketing materials is followed up with a one-hour consultation wherein he recommends specific improvements to the online business.

His guarantee is simple. This is what he tells his clients.

"After listening to my recommendations for 15 minutes, we will pause and I will ask you if you think I am providing advice worth more than my fee. If you answer no, I will not charge you a penny, and we'll still be friends."

His business is flourishing.

A common and very effective guarantee is to offer a bonus item with each purchase. Buyers are told, "You must be 100 percent delighted. If for any reason you are not, simply return your purchase for a prompt refund. No questions asked. The bonus is yours to keep."

Follow up to stand out.

Given the high volume of e-mail flowing into most in-boxes, your follow-up note may not get read. To avoid being overlooked, use your prospect's first name in the subject line. Example: "Bob, here's the summary you requested." Keep your e-mail short. Most buyers, already dealing with information overload, are not inclined to wade through volumes of product data along with your company's history and mission statement. Summarize your discussion and provide links in case they want more information.

Remember to proofread before you hit send. Spelling and grammatical errors in follow-up letters can be a real buyer turnoff.

Some marketers are rediscovering the power of regular mail. Consider following up your initial e-mail with information delivered via regular mail. Include your business card along with your brochure, report, or product spec sheets. It doesn't matter if the prospect has already received this information electronically. The main purpose in using regular mail is to beat the e-mail "fatigue factor" and stay in touch with your prospect.

Power tip: Write a very brief personalized note on the front of the envelope. Example: "Mary, I enjoyed our conversation. Enclosed is a hard copy of the information you requested." Call a few days later to confirm receipt and renew your conversation.

Would you like a table for two?

Knowing how strong the demand is for your product is valuable information and difficult to determine without research. A restaurant consultant developed a fascinating strategy for determining demand.

He goes to a client restaurant on Friday and Saturday nights at 6 p.m. and monitors the wait time to be seated for the next four hours. If the time to be seated consistently exceeds 15 minutes for a month, he advises his client to raise the price of entrees across the board by one dollar. If the wait time continues to exceed 15 minutes for more than two months, he advises the client to raise the prices of the entrees by yet another dollar.

He maintains that monitoring the time it takes for diners to be seated is a very accurate indicator of what the market will bear. He suggests that wait times should not be made too short. The goal of this strategy is to make more money and not shorten wait times. In fact, maintaining a healthy wait time is a good thing because the restaurant's bar stays busier. Have you ever heard, "If you'll have a seat at the bar, I'll call you when your table is ready"?

Real-world research means money in the bank.

Put it in their hands.

Despite the ever-growing importance of the Internet as a marketing tool, don't overlook old-fashioned direct mail. Depending on what you are selling, it can work very well.

Direct mail gives buyers, who have been burned out by a deluge of electronic marketing messages, something to hold in their hands.

Direct mail has a greater chance of working well if:

* It is a well-written piece that has graphic punch.
* The piece has been tested and proven to pull well.
* It is easy for the recipient to place an order because you have included all the needed ordering information.
* The direct mail piece is sent to a highly targeted group. Make certain the list you use is large enough so that, if your targeted mailing generates profits, you can roll it out to a larger group.

Caution: if a piece works well, resist the urge to "make it better" by making changes or additions. Don't change a word.

My most important advice is to find a top-notch direct mail professional to handle all aspects of your campaign. Such professionals aren't cheap, but forget the idea of saving money by doing it in-house. You won't save anything.

Build a database.

A large, clean, targeted marketing database is the queen on the chess-board of business.

Start building your database on day one. It can make the difference between your company soaring or crashing.

A good database allows you to keep in touch with your customers and prospects. Your database also lets you target certain segments with marketing messages of particular interest to that subgroup. It's an invaluable tool for testing offers and prices. Your list can be used to instantly create buzz and drive visitors to your website to check out a new product or make a purchase.

Following are a few database tips.

To build a database, you need a strong rationale for people to sign up. Think free. Few people will opt in to your database unless there is something in it for them. Some sites have "members only" pages which require a prospect to create a free account to access the content. Others offer a free subscription to a newsletter or a regular report. Some sites offer something as mundane as free product updates and notifications of special deals. Your home page should always invite visitors to sign up. However, the more information you request from the registrant, the fewer sign-ups you'll receive. It's important to always ensure complete privacy and state that personal information will never be sold or traded.

You can buy or rent databases to help you build your own. However, be very careful. The database industry is filled with fraudulent companies. When you see ads offering to send e-mails to a couple of million people, run the other way. Social media, trade shows, and advertising can be effective for getting subscribers.

You'll need an ongoing subscriber acquisition plan. Databases grow old quickly. Expect to lose 20 percent of your subscribers each year. Your subscriber sign-ups must be ongoing to make up for the loss.

Attract visitors with a splashy sign-up/subscription form on your home page. Make sure *free* is the first thing they see.

You scratch my back and . . .

I have e-mail trade agreements with dozens of similarly targeted businesses. This is a low-cost and very effective way to grow your sales.

Our company e-mails companies on our database on behalf of a partner in exchange for an e-mail on our behalf to those on our partner's database. Neither partner has any hard costs. An adjustment is made for any disparity in the size of the databases.

Databases are not actually traded; only the e-mail broadcasts are exchanged. Your right to do this should be given to you in terms of the privacy agreement subscribers acknowledge when they opt in to your list.

Here are a couple of caveats to keep in mind.

Do not make this agreement with any company you do not know and trust. The ideal co-op marketing partner is one with a good reputation and a large database of loyal customers. Never e-mail an offer to your list that is even slightly inappropriate. I won't mail for another company unless it offers a guarantee to the buyer, for example. Make sure your partner's list is 100 percent opt-in.

Also determine that your e-mail will be sent only on a Tuesday, Wednesday, or Thursday because response levels drop on days other than these.

Send the persuasive letter.

The creative act is like writing a letter. A letter is a project; you don't sit down to write a letter unless you know what you want to say and to whom you want to say it. —LUKAS FOSS, AMERICAN COMPOSER

Having spent several decades in direct mail, studying business letters is one of my favorite subjects. I have written hundreds of business and prospecting letters that reached several hundred million prospects. I am shocked almost daily by the rank amateurism of ill-crafted business letters that insult intelligent prospects. I expect a badly written letter from those who are peddling blue pills or to inform me that I'm a beneficiary of the will of a dearly departed distant relative in Malta. However, I receive dozens of letters weekly from legitimate, established businesses that apparently think that a desired response can be generated by cheesy letters.

If you write a business letter that you hope will persuade a potential buyer or an affiliate prospect, here's a little tutorial:

* *Get to the point; state your business.* Open by telling readers why you are writing to them. A letter that begins with, "My name is Bob Smith" is poor form. The reader will see your name at the end of the letter. It's even worse if after opening a letter by stating your name, you continue with, "I am the Vice President of Business Development for Songer Software, a provider of business productivity products."

    Let's see, Bob. You've given us your name, your title, your company's name, and a brief description of what it does, but you still haven't told us why you're writing nor have you given us a reason to continue reading. Avoid the introductory preamble, and get right to the point. Tell the reader why you are writing and immediately transition into the central benefit for the reader. If appropriate, use a bulleted list of benefits.

* *Personalize.* A sales letter that begins, "Dear Retailer" or "Dear Software Engineer" immediately informs readers that they have received a form letter and should expect a sales pitch to follow.

Always personalize letters with the recipient's first or last name in the salutation. Never use a first and last name together as in "Dear Robert Swanson." The only people who call others by their first and last name are mothers scolding their children. Your letter should begin with, "Dear Mr. Swanson" or "Dear Robert." I greatly prefer the informal use of the first name. If you are sending an e-mail, use the person's name in the subject line.

* *Keep it clean.* Obviously you'll check for spelling errors and grammatical mistakes. Also look carefully for homophones that may slip into the text. These will not be found by your software's spell-check tool. Common examples of homophones are "your" instead of "you're" and "then" instead of "than." "Break" and "brake" are sometimes confused, too. After composing your letter, take a break and come back to it later to see what you may have missed. I try to get a second person to read my letters because I often get too close to what I've written and don't see the most obvious errors.

* *Keep it authentic.* Write in your own voice. Let your personality show through. Write your letter as if you were writing to an intelligent yet uninformed friend. Keep it simple. Don't use stilted business language. Avoid jargon, "corporate speak," and technical terms. These are all turnoffs for the average reader. Keep your sentences short. Avoid humor or irony. Use *you, yours,* and *yourself,* and limit the use of *me, us, ours,* and *we.*

* *Keep it brief.* Shakespeare wrote that, "Brevity is the soul of wit." It is also the soul of business letters. Always remember that the purpose of a business letter is to give the reader a compelling reason to respond along with the means to do so. Generally speaking, the fewer words used to accomplish this, the better.

* *Close with instructions to the reader.* Tell readers precisely what action you want them to take. Don't close your letter with a vague

statement such as, "I'll call you in a few days to tell you more and answer any questions you may have." Whether you want readers to fill out a card and return it to you by mail or ask them to click on a link to your website to respond to your e-mail, tell them to do it right away. Use a PS that restates a benefit along with the call to action.

✳ *Don't get cute with your sign-off.* When you sign your letters with "Best regards" or "Sincerely," you can't go wrong. A closing such as, "Onward and upward!" is hokey if you don't know the recipient. I exempt the world-renowned motivator Zig Ziglar from this rule because his signature, "I'll see you at the top" is so closely associated with his motivational work. Lately I've seen a trend developing in business letters where the author signs off simply with the word "Best." "Best regards" and "Best wishes" are fine, but I can't understand the use of "Best" by itself. Best what?

Cut marketing last.

During the Great Depression, sales of all products slumped. Ford Motor Company, which was the leading manufacturer of automobiles in the country, made the decision to cut back on its advertising and marketing budget. Ford was selling 10 vehicles for every Chevrolet sold.

Chevrolet made the decision to expand its advertising and marketing expenses during the downturn. At the end of the depression, Chevrolet had left Ford in the dust and emerged as the largest automobile manufacturer in the world.

Clichés sell.

Buzzwords and clichés are stock in trade. There's nothing wrong with them. —MICHAEL NESMITH, AMERICAN SONGWRITER

Well-educated, literary types cringe when they read cliché-ridden advertising copy. However, clichés sell. Terms such as, "We will not be undersold," "Limited-time offer," "Don't miss this deal," "Free gift" (the fact that all gifts are free, doesn't stop the copywriter), "We'll beat any offer," "Nobody beats our prices," and "Only a few left in stock at this price" are like fingernails being drawn across a blackboard for English professors. Be that as it may. If the advertising contained less effusive and better-written copy, it would not work as well.

Clichés sell. If they didn't, they would not be so widely used.

Forget image advertising.

Big businesses advertise to create name recognition or branding. This is done to drive future sales and to own "mind share" with the general public. Unless you are in a league with Nike or Chanel, it is not smart for a small business to emulate big businesses. Small business advertising needs to have one thing in mind—to produce sales. Your goal is to sell, not to create awareness. The best small business's advertisement always includes a compelling reason to buy, such as a needed benefit, a special price or bonus, a call to action, and an easy way for customers to complete the purchase.

Also, consider reducing the size of your ad, so you can run it more often. Short ads can be powerful if the offer is right.

To show or stay home.

Trade shows are a holdover from medieval times when merchants and entertainers came together in a country fair setting. While there certainly are advantages to meeting your prospects face-to-face, how much does it cost you to do this? How many of your prospective buyers are actually at the show?

While trade shows can be excellent ways to meet or reach new clients, it may not be as great an opportunity as you think. If you factor in the cost of registration, travel, food, and lodging, plus the interruption to work flow, you might be surprised at the cost of attending a three-day show. You may be able to use that money to reach far more prospective clients by other means.

Of course, there are benefits to attending trade shows that may outweigh the cost. They are a good place to make business alliances with companies similar to yours and get a read on what your competitors are doing. Whether you choose to go or not go, always go with a plan that outlines your objectives and how you will achieve them.

Tell them a story.

Storytelling is the most powerful way to put ideas into the world today. — ROBERT MCKEE, EDUCATOR

Advertising and marketing messages are everywhere. A tidal wave of them inundates us day in and day out. Because of the sheer volume, most are tuned out. Only a small fraction of ads and marketing messages break through the clutter.

Clever direct marketers, who are continually looking for ways to be heard above the background noise, have found that they can successfully engage buyers by telling a story.

Any good story must have drama. The ideal story should be true and have a happy ending. Short stories work better than long ones. The sales pitch should be at the end.

I e-mailed the following story to a list of business owners, CEOs, sales managers, and sales representatives. The subject line read, "I hate firing people." It's a subject line to which people in all segments of the list could relate. Whether you are firing someone or being fired yourself, it is always a painful experience. This story tells how that painful experience was avoided.

The following letter, which recounts a true story, pulled extremely well. The purpose of my byline is to establish that the reader is about to read a story rather than just another sales pitch.

I Hate Firing People

BY MICHAEL DALTON JOHNSON

I hate firing people. I especially hate firing a salesperson who is working hard but not closing sales.

A year ago I found myself facing that dreaded situation. We had hired a young woman to sell advertising. She took training, understood the product, and had a high call volume. She was hardworking and enthusiastic . . . but she wasn't closing any sales.

Hoping her sales would improve, I put off firing her. However, the fateful day finally came. I had her termination letter in my desk drawer and called her into my office. She came in bright-eyed, smiling, and full of energy. I immediately knew I couldn't fire her. Instead, we discussed the problems she was encountering. I didn't have any real answers.

After the meeting, I asked my managing editor, who works with dozens of sales training experts, who she could recommend to help. I smiled at her quick response when she immediately gave me a name.

We ordered the recommended training and a few days after completing the program our nonperforming salesperson started booking orders! Her sales volume continued to grow impressively.

Magic? No, real-world sales knowledge.

A pitch for the training program followed. Sales were good.

Resist using humor in your advertising.

Unless you are in the same league as national television advertisers, you are far better served putting a specific offer and a call to action in your advertising. Relying on humor probably won't generate as many sales.

Keep it personal.

Your letters and marketing materials are always read by an individual. They should use your reader's name and "you" liberally.

Use the words *we, our, us,* and *I* sparingly. Your message should be about the reader, not you. This is an especially important rule to follow in the opening paragraph of a letter. By using the word "you" along with their name, a bond is created with readers, and your letter is much more likely to be read in its entirety.

Avoid phrases such as, "Our users enjoy significant savings with our product." They won't resonate with the reader. It is far better to begin with "You will enjoy . . ."

Good business communications are friendly and written as if for an intelligent friend. Keep it personal.

Do your homework.

A father and son from my hometown were considering buying a small but very popular take-out restaurant. They planned to use it as a model for a regional fast-food chain. They knew that with any cash business it is easy to "cook the books" by simply adding out-of-pocket cash to your receipts and booking and depositing the artificially enhanced total.

They were suspicious of the owner's sales figures, so after determining the average amount spent by each patron, they staked out the restaurant. Much like a police stakeout, they parked a van, with a clear view of the restaurant's entrance, and counted the number of patrons who visited each day. They did this for a week. Then they asked the restaurant owner for that week's sales numbers.

The owner's sales numbers matched, within a few percentage points, the number of patrons they had counted multiplied by the average sale price they had predetermined.

They purchased the business.

Overkill? Probably not if you are using the performance of one restaurant as the basis for building an entire chain.

How is your company perceived?

How your company is perceived is an issue central to your success. Does the face you present to prospective customers create expectations and a perception of quality and value? If not, you have a problem.

Say you enter a restaurant and the waitress looks over her shoulder and says, "Sit anywhere you want." The tables are set with paper placemats, flatware, salt and pepper, ketchup, and hot sauce. You immediately know what to expect regarding food quality, service, and price.

Now, let's say that you enter a restaurant and are greeted by a well-groomed host or hostess. The tables have cloth tablecloths, porcelain plates, and fresh flowers. A piano is being played in the corner. You immediately have expectations of gourmet food, attentive service, and a price to match the experience.

While this is a very obvious way in which buyers perceive things, customers form perceptions from more cues than you might imagine. Are your sales and customer service personnel well trained? Do your website and personnel reflect a high degree of professionalism?

Seeing is believing.

The old adage, "A picture is worth a thousand words," is especially true in marketing. In fact, most products simply can't be sold without images. (Can you imagine trying to sell clothing without pictures?)

To be effective, a picture must evoke emotions. A new casino might send a letter to every household within a 20-mile radius describing the facility and all it has to offer. It might include special offers and inducements, but it is not likely to receive much response. If, however, it were to mail a full-color brochure with a collage of photos of the facility showing a gourmet buffet, excited people celebrating jackpots, stacks of chips, bright lights, rows of slot machines and gaming tables crowded with people, it will have created an exciting party atmosphere. Evocative photos fire imaginations and emotions. The following weekend the casino's parking lot will be full.

Always look for that evocative picture that perfectly captures the spirit of your marketing message. You'll know it when you see it. When you find it, that picture will be worth many times a thousand words.

To act or not to act.

"Take action now" is advice given in nearly every entrepreneurial book you read or seminar you attend. It's good advice—most of the time. Why wait for that ideal job candidate to get hired before you call? Why wait to roll out a mailing that has been tested and shown to really pull in the orders? In fact, why wait for a business opportunity of any kind to fade away?

Since the advice to act now is so pervasive, it's not surprising that the entrepreneurial world is filled with people who would far rather act now than wait for more information.

There are times when you should wait. Not acting does not mean that you have lost control of a situation or are showing poor leadership. It simply means that you are not being swept along by emotion and that you are rationally and objectively looking to make a decision that will lead to success.

When no decision is necessary, it is necessary that no decision be made.

When you feel something needs to be done, it is smart to consider what might happen if you don't act. Depending on the circumstances, it may be wise to wait for events to unfold and to have all the details before acting. This is also a time when entrepreneurial instinct coupled with common sense will serve you well.

6 | THE INTERNET

The information superhighway is a dirt road that won't be paved over until 2025.

— SUMNER REDSTONE, CEO OF
VIACOM/BLOCKBUSTER

BACK IN THE EARLY 1990s my business partner mentioned this new thing called the Internet. My response, as I recall, was perfunctory. I probably said something like, "Oh really? That sounds interesting." Shortly thereafter the Internet started getting media attention, and businesses began paying attention.

It wasn't long before entrepreneurial companies saw the opportunities and started staking their claims. The Internet quickly revolutionized existing industries and gave birth to new ones.

Today, millions of players from stay-at-home parents to Fortune 500 companies are doing business online.

Internet marketing technology is growing exponentially. It is said that one dog year equals seven human years. With the Internet, the equation is much different. Because of its mind-boggling rate of growth, I estimate an Internet year to be somewhere around three months!

For better or worse, the Internet now permeates our culture and our very lives. While the Internet is an incredible sales and marketing tool, it is a very dangerous place. Buyers are understandably cautious. Misrepresentations seem to be the rule. Scams abound. Clueless "experts" offer to make you a millionaire overnight. Others dangle a variety of "too good to be true" rip-off offers designed to separate you from your hard-earned cash. You've seen their bogus promises: overnight weight loss, instant stimulus checks, miracle cures. The list goes on. On top of all this, you can add tracking cookies, phishing, viruses, spam, spyware, and Trojan horses. It's no wonder that buyers are wary. Wary buyers make it difficult to establish a legitimate online business.

Unless you are a professional Internet marketer, resist trying to develop a comprehensive Internet marketing strategy on your own.

Keeping pace is a full-time job which may not be the best use of your time and talents. Probably the smartest thing you can do to harness the power of the Net is to realize how little you know and get expert help.

Unless you are in a league with Macy's or Amazon, or well known within your industry, an essential job of your website is to overcome buyer caution. Post a list of customer referrals, publish bios, offer a solid guarantee of satisfaction, and have a strong privacy notice. While you can put all kinds of these commonsense "credibility enhancers" on your website, a simple thing like including your street address and phone number really increases buyer confidence.

Whatever you do, unless you are a big insurance company giving instant online car insurance quotes, do not require potential buyers to submit an e-mail inquiry form and wait for your response. I don't want to start a business relationship with an assignment from the seller. I refuse to spend my time filling out intrusive online forms in order to get a call back.

Could we at least say hello before I tell you my time frame to purchase, number of employees, and annual sales? I also don't want to leave a voice message and wait for a return call when you get around to it. I am the buyer. It's my agenda—not yours.

Want my business? Tell me who you are and talk to me!

It's the same game but different equipment.

People started racing cars shortly after cars were invented. It was the same game as racing horses, but the equipment had changed. The Internet is the new equipment for growing a business, but the rules of the game have remained the same: offer a product or service, tell prospective buyers about it, have a means of delivering the product or service, and have a way of receiving payment.

Buyers are motivated by the same things as they were 100 years ago. The only thing that has changed is the method for reaching them.

The Internet per se will not make you a success. Understanding how to appeal to the needs and desires of human beings will.

Enter nerdvana.

The exponential acceleration of technology gives you new ways of marketing your service or product. Because of the rapid advance of technology, your marketing plan may be obsolete in six months.

Because of the ever-changing nature of technology, it is a good idea to employ, what I call, technical marketing nerds. These are usually young, tech-savvy people who know the nuts-and-bolts tricks for getting your marketing message out.

You know these guys and gals. (You may be one of them yourself.) They are the scary smart people in T-shirts, Levi's, and scruffy running shoes. They have spent their young lives immersed in the changing technical world, and their understanding and mastery of it seems to come naturally.

The demand for such minds is great. Get your nerds early on—before they become millionaires on their own.

Publish a newsletter.

The new information technology—Internet and e-mail—have practically eliminated the physical costs of communications.

—PETER DRUCKER

A newsletter is a great way to engage and stay in touch with your buyers and prospects. A successful newsletter is lively and focused on your readers' specific needs and interests. However, depending on your readership, you may want to sprinkle in a few nonrelated editorial features that entertain, such as trivia questions or interesting facts. Contests, polls, and brief mentions of free "no strings" deals you're offering are also good ways to engage readers.

Keep articles brief. You won't hold your readers' attention with long articles. Readers want industry news, case histories, solutions, and product reviews presented in a lively and engaging style.

Of course, there are exceptions to these guidelines. I receive one newsletter from a large company's CEO which breaks all the rules. His monthly newsletter is mostly his personal reflections on subjects as varied as space exploration, home gardening, and his experiences in buying a new car. He occasionally throws in a humorous rant on subjects such as traffic, poor service, or current cultural trends. His product and industry news is mentioned only as footnotes. Judging from the several hundred thousand subscribers to the newsletter, this formula works for him. Caution: this style of newsletter requires a very gifted writer.

Make your newsletter's look, voice, and personality distinct and appropriate to the industry it serves. I can't imagine a newsletter for neurosurgeons being as breezy and chatty as one for salespeople.

A company newsletter is definitely something where the saying, "Go big or go home" applies.

Your newsletter is a promotional tool with the long-term marketing goals of broadening your reach and establishing you as an authoritative industry voice. Reaching these goals gives you a significant competitive edge. Keep in mind that you will quickly lose your audience and your credibility by making your newsletter one big sales pitch. Again, keep your articles short and interesting and, above all, useful for your readers.

If you create articles that really score with your readers, they will get forwarded to others. This added benefit extends your reach and brings in more subscribers. I published one article that "went viral" on the Internet, and I picked up 2,200 new subscribers to my newsletter in one week. It's a good idea to continue articles on your home page to increase site traffic. A short index of past articles with links to them is also a good idea.

Don't have the time? It takes more time than you might imagine to write and edit content. Because of this, it is probably best to begin with a monthly rather than a weekly newsletter. It may be smart to hire an experienced freelance writer. You provide the ideas and direction, and the freelancer does the hard work of pulling it all together and giving you polished and compelling copy.

To bravely go.

There is a lot of unwarranted fear about marketing via broadcast e-mail. Any company has the unfettered right to send e-mail to anyone it wants as long as it follows the rules governing this activity.

I once recommended broadcast e-mail to a small specialty software company that was introducing a new product. The company had recently purchased a database of 50,000 prospects for use by its telemarketers. I discovered that the database also included e-mail addresses.

I suggested that we test a few thousand names with the company's standard offer of a free 30-day demo version.

I was presenting this idea to the marketing group when the marketing manager became visibly agitated. Finally she blurted, "This is a bad idea! Unsolicited broadcast e-mailing is a form of corporate vandalism, and I don't think we can afford to get a bad reputation with our customers."

She went on to say that she was convinced it wouldn't work but could offer no facts to back up her opinion. Despite her passionate protests, management decided to do a test e-mail to 5,000 names.

Three days after the e-mail went out, I got a call from the company's president. The firm had generated 43 orders and 2 complaints.

E-mails went to the rest of the database the following week. Ultimately, millions of dollars' worth of products were sold via broadcast e-mail.

Cast a wide net.

Low-cost access to millions of buyers which is possible via the Internet sounds like every entrepreneur's dream. It's not.

Because there's a lot of fish in the Internet sea (including a lot of sharks), e-mail is a very powerful tool for sales and business growth, but e-mailing must be done right. The ability to write effective e-mails is money in the bank.

Volumes have been written about effective e-mail marketing. It's a complicated subject that should be part of your ongoing education.

Here is a short tutorial to help you create e-mail that will interest your prospects and drive sales:

* Show them the money.
* Include the biggest benefit to the buyer in your all-important opening paragraph.

* Get to the point. Make sure the first paragraph of your business e-mail gives the recipient a clear picture of what your communication is about. Don't waste time with a long-winded opening. No one is interested in you or your company's history.

* Keep it easy to understand.

* Do not assume that everyone knows your industry's jargon. Dump it. Avoid abbreviations and acronyms. Never use all caps for a word or phrase in an attempt to emphasize its importance.

* Keep your sentences and paragraphs short.

* Keep your message crystal clear, complete, accurate, and brief. Most people are deluged with spam and unsolicited e-mail every day. To ensure that recipients read your e-mail, keep it lively, short, and to the point.

* Avoid tricks and gimmicks.

* Your subject line should not be misleading. Never begin an e-mail with, "My name is . . ." People opening your e-mail are not the least interested in your name. They are interested in why you have e-mailed them. They will see your name when they reach the bottom of the text.

* Personalize. It is important to use the recipient's name in the salutation. I prefer informal greetings such as Hello Susan or Hi John. However, there may be times when a more formal salutation is appropriate.

* Avoid rhetorical questions.

* Asking questions such as, "Do you want to save 50 percent on your printing costs?" is both silly and salesy.

* Give them a reason to act.

* Close with a strong rationale for the action you want the recipient to take.

* Signing off. A simple "Best regards" or "Very truly yours," followed by your name suffices.

✴ Your e-mail represents you and your organization and should always include your name, address, city, state, zip code, phone and fax numbers, and e-mail address. This makes you and your company look professional, legitimate, and accessible.

✴ Review the message to be sure it is deliverable.

✴ Don't get filtered out. Use an online spam check service. It's free.

Internet dollars.

Because of the low cost of acquisition, a dollar earned online is worth two dollars earned offline.

Internet marketers increasingly are turning to continuity programs. They will sell you a program that delivers something each month, at which point they will bill your credit card. Continuity programs have a lot of advantages for marketers because they require only one sale. Once that sale is made, income is locked in for the life of the contract.

Your success will not go unnoticed.

A successful hunt on the African savanna immediately attracts a host of scavengers and predators wanting to share in the kill. Similarly, success on the Internet quickly catches the attention of others who want their share. These will include those who will grab variations of your web address or who roll out cheesey knockoffs of your product. There is really no way to avoid this except to move fast in the market and protect your property rights legally.

Avoid the fatigue factor.

If you market to a specific niche, especially if you are marketing via e-mail, you run the risk of creating a fatigue factor in your prospect database. The fatigue factor kicks in when every e-mail you send is a sales pitch. In short order, many of the recipients of your e-mail won't bother to open them.

A proven way to avoid the fatigue factor is to regularly send out articles that do not sell but rather provide interesting information to your prospects. It can be a news item, an interesting case history, or observations written by an industry authority. What you send should be brief, easy to read, and fast paced. Resist the urge to sell anything.

Providing useful and interesting content establishes a relationship between you and your prospects. Your credibility grows when your prospects realize that their relationship with you has perks and is not based strictly on marketing your product to them.

Word of mouth is now word of Internet.

Word of mouth has long been held to be the best and least expensive form of advertising. Creating a buzz to get people talking about your business might be a good idea for a local restaurant or boutique. But if you're doing business on the Internet, it's an especially good idea. The Internet creates word of mouth on steroids!

My buddy, who had launched a novelty product, called me and excitedly said, "I had over 60,000 visitors to my website yesterday!" A major online news site had published a small article with a picture of his product. That did it. His site continued to receive a large volume of visitors for several months, and smaller sites and blogs featured his product. While the craze for his product burned out quickly, as many novelty products do, he made a lot of money. He never spent a dime on advertising.

Load 'em up.

Picture a cattle chute that is large at the entrance and becomes progressively narrower until the cattle being driven have nowhere to go except into the truck or boxcar.

Direct marketing on the Internet is similar. Potential buyers are first attracted to your site by marketing that promises a benefit, arouses curiosity, or perhaps offers something for free. Once there, they are sent to a landing page, and the chute narrows. The landing page sets forth the benefits of ownership and directs them to place their orders. When they click on the order button, the chute narrows further, but they are not onboard yet. When they have arrived at the order page, it's important that they feel comfortable about ordering. Many buyers are lost at the order page because they don't feel secure about proceeding. It's important to always restate your guarantee and have a security logo displayed on your order page. Once they submit their order, they are onboard.

Recently I wrote an e-mail and designed a landing page for a client to get registrants for his webinar. He put the landing page for the webinar up on his site. When I checked it, I found that there were 17 links that took the visitor away from the webinar page. The only link on that page should have been the one that took them to webinar registration. The 17 links included a complete site navigation bar, offers on other products, and an invitation to sign up for his free newsletter.

I explained to him that all the links would distract buyers from what he wanted them to do and could cut his response significantly. He wasn't a student of buyer behavior, but I finally convinced him to remove the links. The webinar was well attended.

7 | WORKING SMARTER

The person who is waiting for something to turn up might start with their shirt sleeves.

— GARTH HENRICHS, WRITER

WHETHER YOUR COMPANY is up and running or you are just putting the finishing touches on your business plan, it's time to roll up your sleeves. It's also time to come to a keen appreciation for the value of your time and ways to conserve it. You won't get much done each day unless you monitor your time and recognize the things that are using it.

There is wisdom in the old business cliché that advises us to, "Work smarter, not harder." It's advice that is much easier said than done.

Hard work will get you ahead. If you concentrate your efforts on reaching a goal, you will undoubtedly achieve more than if you approach a task halfheartedly. However, even though you are putting in the hours and working hard, you may not be working effectively and you may not ultimately reach your goal.

This chapter gives you some practical tips on working smarter.

Think focus and flexibility. Focus on your goals, but have the flexibility to take advantage of new opportunities. Clarify your vision. Assemble a great support group from outside your organization. Make sure you have a hard-nosed advisor. Don't get caught up in bureaucratic rules and procedures. Your goal is to grow profits, not paperwork. Get paid faster. Get a discount on nearly everything you buy. Reinvent your business from time to time. Work smarter.

Observe the 18-month rule.

Even though you may have no plans to sell, run your business as if you were going to sell for top dollar in 18 months.

This is an important mindset for you to maintain because business buyers want the same thing you do—a profitable business.

Business buyers will understandably look first at a company's cash flow and profitability. If the bottom line is healthy, only then will they look for the potential for future profits.

Observation of the 18-month rule will put your decisions in a new perspective and your focus on growing profits.

You'll find that there are surprisingly few times when you need to deviate from this rule.

Start it cold.

Defy the downturn and start a business during an economic slump? Are you kidding?

It's understandable why many people would prefer to wait out an economic downturn before launching a business.

However, starting a business during tough times may be an excellent idea.

During the recession of the 1990s, I started two companies that flourished. With one, I was lucky enough to catch the very beginning of the computer revolution. We sold informational products that allowed businesses to save time and money. The almost immediate return on their investment drove our sales and profits.

During tough economic times cash-short businesses cut back on purchasing big-ticket items and look for ways to reduce operating expenses. If you are offering a product or service that saves people money, you will get their attention.

Consumers understandably curb spending on big-ticket retail items during a recession. They too are looking for ways to save money, but they still want entertainment and inspiration and are willing to pay for it. During the Depression, movie attendance, which was already high, soared. In Chicago, in the 1930s, theaters had enough seats to accommodate half the city's population.

If you have the right idea, a weak economy may be precisely the right time to launch your business. Confront uncertainty with ingenuity and don't wait for the tide to turn. Be part of the reason why it is turning.

Red hot is risky.

Start-ups are especially risky businesses in red hot markets. Huh?

Remember when cigars were all the rage? Fashion models puffed stogies on magazine covers, and well-known actors extolled the pleasures of a well-rolled cigar on the inside pages. You couldn't escape the smoke. Soon there was a proliferation of small cigar stores popping up in strip malls across the country. Most of them, which were very expensive to stock with fine cigars and equip with walk-in humidors, are now boarded up. The fad is gone, and so is their money.

Every year or two a similar craze comes on the scene. About the time the wave is cresting, people start jumping in and the ride down is quick and costly.

Have breakfast with entrepreneurs.

You'll get more practical nuts-and-bolts advice from other entrepreneurs than you will from any other source. They're dealing with the same challenges you are. They have often found solutions to problems that you haven't yet solved. They refer you to new business or direct you to vendors that can save you money.

With this in mind, I started what I called an entrepreneurs' breakfast club. I invited area businesspeople from varied industries to meet each week to talk business. The meetings were informal roundtable discussions where a participant could throw out a question to the group. Some would talk about new developments at their company, and others would ask for referrals to vendors. There were no speeches and no agenda. Attendance was limited to eight. The information flowed, and the hour went by quickly.

The real-world advice I received at these breakfasts was literally money in the bank.

Best doesn't always finish first.

A good basic selling idea, involvement and relevancy, of course, are as important as ever, but in the advertising din of today, unless you make yourself noticed and believed, you ain't got nothing.
— LEO BURNETT, ADVERTISING EXECUTIVE

The most successful businesses are not always the ones that offer the best product or service. Sometimes entrepreneurial success is driven primarily by marketing acumen. Some companies with a so-so product gain a significant advantage over the competition by simply being the best at selling themselves.

However, if you offer a superior product or service and link that with superior marketing, you will have an unstoppable combination.

Never ask a barber if you need a haircut.

If you ask a mason what material you should use to build your house, it is a safe bet that he will tell you to use bricks. Ask a programmer what software you should use to do a particular job, and chances are very good he will recommend the one he is most familiar with, which may not be the least expensive or best tool for what you need. The solution he recommends may include expensive features you do not need and will never use.

Always seek objective advice before committing to a purchase. Someone who has a financial interest in your buying decision is never your best source of advice. Online user reviews are an excellent source of information as are articles from trusted publishers.

Talk to the power behind the throne.

You may find yourself negotiating with someone who seemingly has the power to make a deal with you, but who really doesn't.

I was in talks with the owner of a small magazine company about creating and implementing a large subscriber acquisition plan. We met several times, had come to terms, and were ready to close the deal. We arranged to meet to work out the final details.

Our meeting had just started when an older gentleman walked in carrying a plate of cookies.

"Your aunt wanted me to drop these off," he said.

She introduced him to me as her Uncle Nate. She asked if anyone would like coffee to go with the cookies. Uncle Nate said he could really use a cup. He pulled up a chair as she left to get the coffee.

"So what are you and Judy working on?" he asked.

I told him we were launching a plan to get more subscribers.

"Oh, that sounds interesting," he said. He continued to ask questions. He seemed to be making polite conversation.

I'm sure you have guessed where this story is going. I learned later that Uncle Nate was financing the company and had final approval on our deal. He was interviewing me, but didn't want his niece to look like she didn't have the authority to act on her own.

I later learned that Uncle Nate was the retired owner of a large manufacturing plant. I've always wondered if the cookies were his idea.

East meets west.

First, make yourself a reputation for being a creative genius. Second, surround yourself with partners who are better than you are.

— DAVID OGILVY, ADVERTISING
EXECUTIVE

I am optimistic. I tend to be a dreamer, a person who sees possibilities and ideas and imagines wonderful outcomes. I confess that I don't want to be bothered too much with details or minutia. Early in my business career, I recognized that I'm not very good with numbers or financial analysis.

I can read a profit and loss statement and a balance sheet, and I can understand financial projections, but I don't want to be the guy preparing them or keeping the records to create them. I don't have much talent for looking at parts of things. I want to see the big picture. This is a characteristic of a right-brained person.

When I teamed up, quite by chance, with a partner who had a strong accounting background, good things began to happen. He was a left-brain personality. He was extremely numbers-oriented and had great analytical talents. Although we both knew it was a match made in heaven, we continually annoyed each other.

We went on to create a successful business together. Whether you're right-brained or left-brained, remember that when you join with your counterpart, you create a whole brain. Beyond the ideal left-brain/right-brain thing, partners must of course have a lot in common. They should have the same sense of business ethics and share a common business objective. Shared personality traits such as work ethic, motivation, communication skills, generosity, and energy level are essential in creating that match made in heaven.

Learn to read people.

Body language is a very powerful tool. We had body language before we had speech, and apparently, 80 percent of what you understand in a conversation is read through the body, not the words.

—DEBORAH BULL, ENGLISH
ENTERTAINER

Police detectives, professional poker players, and successful deal makers have one thing in common: they all know how to read people.

At least 80 percent of human communication is nonverbal. Eye movement, posture, arm positioning, hand gestures, facial expressions, voice inflection, and other subtle and unintentionally sent messages can be read and interpreted. Plenty of learning resources on this subject exist. Take advantage of them. Your ability to read people pays big dividends in your professional and personal life.

Beyond business, there are dozens of life situations in which knowledge of body language pays off. Whether you're making a major purchase, interviewing, dealing with coworkers, or even with those at the dinner table, it is a very useful skill.

Are you being lied to?

I'm certainly not an expert on reading body language, but I have made it a point to learn the basic signs that tell me I am being lied to. Here are a few things I look for:

If a person doesn't use contractions in his or her speech, it's an indication of lying. When you hear, "I did not do it," instead of, "I didn't do it," chances are that person is fibbing.

Also people offering a theory that removes them from suspicion such as, "I would not take the chocolates. I do not even like chocolate," and then offers an alternative theory, such as, "Maybe the cleaning crew took them," is probably lying.

A change in the tone of voice often also indicates deception.

Tugging at one's collar and crossing one's arms are other obvious indicators.

None of these behaviors viewed separately means much, but, you can rest assured that, if three or more are displayed, it's a pretty safe bet that you are being lied to.

Turnover is desirable.

The only thing worse than losing well-trained people, is having people who are not well-trained, and keeping them.

—DEBORAH DOUGLAS, FOUNDER
OF DOUGLAS GROUP

As your company grows and changes, you need people with different skills from the ones you began with. Author Paul Armer writes: "People become progressively less competent for jobs they once were well equipped to handle."

My view is that their jobs get progressively more complicated, not that people become less competent. Most people know when their job has outgrown their abilities. Often they will fire themselves. If not, help them gracefully move on. Their leaving will accelerate your growth.

However, if you have employees who are motivated and loyal, you will want to invest in training so that they can grow with you as your company grows. Whenever possible, take the good ones with you.

Investors are like cats (and you're probably a dog!).

Just like our feline friends, investors can be a difficult lot—suspicious, wary, finicky, independent, and aloof. If you chase after one, it always runs. If you attempt to coax it, it invariably ignores you. However, if you sit quietly, letting the cat take its time and make up its own mind, before you know it, it's purring on your lap.

Once you have investors' interest, they will naturally want to see well-documented facts and figures rigorously researched and professionally presented. Have the answers to their questions before they ask them. Do not oversell an investor or you will come off as desperate. Simply state the facts and answer questions.

I once was talking with a private investor about funding for an expansion plan. He questioned every number and premise in our plan. Once he was presented with the underlying documentation, he questioned that documentation. Even though our investors were well secured and the business was profitable, the questions went on and on.

I had been jumped through enough hoops and finally had enough. During yet another meeting with him, I smiled, looked him in the eye, and said, "You know, Bob, let's face it. This investment really isn't for you." I added, "I'm sure you can find an opportunity that is better suited to your needs."

I stood up and extended my hand to him and thanked him for his interest. I was essentially kicking him out of my office.

While this was not a sales tactic, it apparently worked like one. The next day he called to tell me he was in. The cat came back.

A valuable business doesn't need you.

The less you are needed to run your company, the more valuable it becomes.

A business that has a solid foothold in the market, a good product, and a great management team that does not require the owner's day-to-day involvement is pure gold. Business buyers are willing to pay top dollar for a company that doesn't require day-to-day management.

As the owner, you can show up for board meetings, be in on strategic decisions, spend six weeks at a time in the south of France, and enjoy the profits of the enterprise.

Beyond its value in the marketplace, such a business is a sparkling gem because you reap the benefits long after your hard work in building it is done.

Losing isn't winning.

Many business gurus point out the wonderful benefits of failure, theorizing that failure gives you a chance to see what you've done wrong and avoid mistakes in your second attempt.

I understand their point, but I have never really liked the idea. Aside from the somewhat dubious benefit that losing helps you learn, I can think of no other possible benefit. In fact, I think losing teaches you to lose and that winning teaches you to win.

Do what you do well.

My grandfather advised me that I would always have work if I could do something well. Whether it is painting houses, cutting hair, or closing deals, if you are good at it, you will always have work. Find your gift.

Is there a reason for joining?

Trade organizations can be a fantastic source of industry intelligence. They also present wonderful networking opportunities. However, look carefully at any organization before you join and be sure that your membership will provide you with bottom-line benefits. Quite often you will find that it does not.

Give yourself a job evaluation.

From time to time sit down with yourself and review your goals and the progress you've made toward achieving them. This should be a more defined and purposeful activity than simple day to day reflection. Set aside 10 or 15 minutes to complete this exercise.

Take a look at your numbers. Evaluate your progress. Take a detached look at where you might have bogged down or gone off track, and rethink your strategies.

Give yourself a score between one and one hundred.

You don't need to take notes or write a plan. At the end of this exercise you will know what you need to do.

Get a first-rate copywriter.

All your written materials, from company brochures to product specification sheets to web content to sales letters and proposals, should absolutely sing. Never allow members of your sales staff to write their own letters. Instead, provide them with well-written form letters that they can modify for each prospect. In order to pull well, letters soliciting prospects must contain very specific elements. Creating them should not be a do-it-yourself project.

Professionally conceived and written letters, web content, and brochures greatly enhance your image and believability with buyers and investors.

Give your copywriter final approval for all written materials coming from your organization. This person should be a gifted marketing copywriter (not an English professor) who can create polished and compelling communications.

Pay people 10 percent more than they're worth.

In business, few things are more expensive than incompetence. By paying more, you will attract higher-caliber employees and keep them for a longer term of service.

Ideas are worthless unless . . .

Nearly everyone has had a "better mouse trap" idea—a cool concept that is sure to electrify the market and rake in huge sales. Such an idea may in fact have enormous potential, but the idea by itself is worthless. For an idea to gain value, it must be accompanied by a way to access the market.

Do your homework. If market research indicates the viability of the idea, then it starts to have value. However, without a plan and a means to bring the idea to market and sell it, it simply remains an idea. If your idea has gone beyond the research stage and test marketing has actually generated cash, the idea becomes golden. It will attract people and money.

Should you buy or build?

Making good decisions is a crucial skill at every level. — PETER DRUCKER

A neighbor of mine, who is a classic car aficionado, went to a large classic car show in Los Angeles. One of the vehicles was a beautiful, fully restored 1955 Ford pickup truck. He struck up a conversation with the owner who asked him if he would like to buy it. My friend told him he couldn't afford it. The owner said, "Make me an offer." My buddy told him that anything he could offer would be far below the value of the vehicle.

"Try me," the owner said.

"Okay," my friend said, "I'll give you five grand."

Without hesitation the owner said, "Sold!"

It turns out that the owner was an attorney who owned a collection of a dozen more classic vehicles. He jokingly told my neighbor that his wife had instructed him not to come home with the truck. To bring a vehicle up to the pristine condition of the truck would have taken months and cost tens of thousands of dollars.

Business sellers often have a far more compelling reason to sell than the truck owner had. Retirement, divorce, a pressing need for cash, and a host of other personal reasons may motivate them.

Depending on the type of business you want, it may be far cheaper to buy it than to start one from scratch. This is especially true if costly equipment is required. When you consider the time and money saved by avoiding recruiting and training a staff, start-up advertising and marketing, acquiring equipment, negotiating a lease, and dealing with regulatory agencies, there may be some real bargains out there. Most sellers include a training period for the new owner as part of the deal.

One caveat: To go this route, you need professional help from an accountant as well as from an attorney who is experienced in business sales. This is no time to skimp. Hire the best and avoid headaches down the road.

Recruit; don't coach.

I enjoy coaching people. It can be very satisfying to see someone increase his or her work skills as a result of coaching. However, recruiting is far more important than coaching.

You would be wise to hire people who don't need extensive coaching. Rewarding as it may be, coaching is not the best use of your time.

It's a false economy to save money on salary by hiring someone without solid experience and then give them on-the-job training. In fact, it's a strategy that can eat up your time and money and take you away from your primary business goals.

If your team needs coaching, it may be cheaper and more effective to bring in an expert coach from time to time.

There's no place like . . . work.

People associate home and homelike surroundings with leisure and a relaxed pace. These are not elements you want to promote in the workplace. Therefore, your workplace should look like an office.

You'll never have all the facts.

Many companies overanalyze. This is a sign of weak leadership. Committees are formed, studies are conducted, accounting is called in, projections are reforecast, outside opinions are sought, meritless changes are recommended, and retesting is undertaken.

The clock keeps ticking. The burn rate goes on. The competition creeps closer. While analysis is essential, don't overdo it. At a certain point, it's time to go with your instincts. And a good leader knows when he or she has reached that point.

I was struggling with a business decision, and I asked an investor, who had helped with the research, for his opinion. He thought for a moment and said that the research had been done to everyone's satisfaction and he would advise me to go forward.

I replied that I didn't feel that I had all the facts. He picked up a pencil off my desk and said, "I could give you months to gather all the facts about this pencil, and you couldn't do it. Sure, you might learn where the wood was grown, where the lead was mined, and the chemical composition of the yellow paint. You might even learn the location of the plantation where the rubber was grown to make the eraser, but I'll bet you wouldn't know the maiden name of the plantation owner's wife's maternal grandmother."

We both laughed, and he smiled and put the pencil back and said, "You'll never have all the facts."

Share opportunities with higher-level managers.

One of the best strategies for retaining key personnel is to share the profits of their departments with them. Rather than paying a straight percentage of profits, I would formulate a bonus plan that accumulates, is paid periodically, and is zeroed out if an employee resigns.

Make sure this is legal where you operate your business.

The sky is not falling.

While serving as director of development for a trade publishing company, a customer service manager sent me a somewhat breathless memo regarding product returns. One of the sentences in the memo was, "People are returning the programming tips manual." Apparently, some customers had complained about the price we were charging, and the customer service manager suggested we lower the price so we would get fewer returns.

I met with her and learned that she had received three returns in one month. During this month we had sold more than a thousand copies of the book. I explained to her that the returns represented a small percentage of sales, but she persisted in magnifying the problem, stating that the reputation of the company was her primary concern.

Of course we didn't lower the price of the book. Ultimately, we sold more than 35,000 copies with 87 returns.

An interesting aside: one of the books returned by the CIO of a very large company had a note affixed to it which read, "Marge, copy this book and return it to the publisher. — Bob." I couldn't help but wonder how many others had done the same thing simply to get their money back. I also think Marge was blowing the whistle on her boss.

Mood follows form.

To create well I have to be in a good mood, happy and cool.
> — MARC NEWSON,
> ENTREPRENEUR

When you feel in winning form, you smile, stand up straight, and walk with confidence. On a gloomy, depressing day, try this: smile, stretch, and strut. Your mood will begin to lighten as your physical actions mimic those of a winner. The same applies to your phone personality. If you sit up straight and smile, you begin to feel self-confident and purposeful. Your voice reflects those qualities, and you will enjoy more successful business conversations.

The more you learn, the more you earn.

The most important advice for anyone who sells for a living is that the more you learn, the more you earn. Make a commitment to your success. Every day invest a little time in sharpening your sales skills. The number-one mistake salespeople make is neglecting their ongoing sales education. No excuses. This doesn't have to be a huge investment of time or money. There are plenty of free or low-cost sales skills improvement resources on the Internet. Get started today.

Expand your vocabulary.

One forgets words as one forgets names. One's vocabulary needs constant fertilizing or it will die. — EVELYN WAUGH, AUTHOR

There is a proven relationship between vocabulary and income. Most successful people have good vocabularies and can express their ideas clearly. Less successful people tend to rely on a limited vocabulary augmented with clichés to get their ideas across. You are taken far more seriously when you can express yourself articulately. Clear and precise language gains you respect and credibility.

Don't bother to learn words that are never used in everyday conversation. The fact that you know the meaning of *popinjay* is not of any value. However, learning one new word a day is money in the bank.

Investigate your buyer.

Before calling that important prospect, go online and do some investigation. Check the person's profile online. Learn a little about his or her background, interests, and education. Then go to his or her company website and read the latest press release. Take a few notes. Armed with this information, you'll have a much better chance of establishing that all-important first contact rapport. This takes only a few minutes and is time well spent. You'll build your relationship with the buyer quicker and have a much better chance of ultimately closing the deal.

Don't make a move unless the fix is in.

You are naturally enthused about your new business. You know you have a great idea, and everyone you talk to agrees with you.

But keep in mind that you may be going down a dead-end road. A surprising number of entrepreneurs who feel that they have a "can't miss" idea dive excitedly into a pool that may have no water in it. They are oblivious to the danger of not knowing the market potential for their idea.

Play like the big boys do. Get the fix in. I'm not talking about bribing politicians; I'm talking about doing your marketing homework and doing it well.

How great is the market for your product or service? It's difficult to determine without research. Talking to a few dozen relatives and friends is not market research.

Getting professional market research is money very well spent. Never commit time and capital to untested ideas.

With money or time, new customers are bought.

The question is, how much will new customers cost you? There are many inexpensive ways to acquire customers—word of mouth being the cheapest of all. Clever advertising, publicity, and promotions are also very effective. You must determine, with a fair degree of accuracy, what your acquisition costs are.

Don't knock the competition.

Sure, you can compare your products to those of the competition. This is a legitimate practice; however, it is very poor business form to give your opinion on the lack of quality of a competitor's product or service.

Your potential customers often view this in a negative light. If they happen to be using your competitor's product and you knock it, it makes them look stupid for having made a bad choice.

There's a big difference between saying your product is superior and saying your competitor's is inferior.

Dressing for success at home.

A neighbor who works from home selling advertising often started his work late because of early morning distractions. He told me that some days he was still in his pajamas at two in the afternoon. He checked his e-mail and visited his social media pages. He spent too much time surfing the web. He procrastinated and didn't feel compelled to get to work and stay working. He would stop in the afternoon to shower and get ready for his wife's return from her job.

His efforts weren't very productive, and he realized that he needed to make changes. He gave it some thought and decided to treat his home office as a place of business. He set a time where he had to be at the "office." He would shower, shave, and dress in business attire before starting work. He cut back on non-work-related activities. He said that his new regimen had a profoundly positive effect on his work. Once he started considering his work a full-time job, his sales increased significantly. His professional solution gave him professional results.

Grow your profits, not your organization.

The following story has been repeated many times: A successful entrepreneur buys an unprofitable and failing business. He fires 50 percent of the executives, slashes operating expenses, and relaunches the product with an aggressive new marketing and sales team. Within a few quarters, the company is enjoying big profits. The entrepreneur is hailed as a genius for doing the obvious. You can be a genius yourself by reinventing your company and not allowing your operation to grow faster than its profits.

Get specific, and stay specific.

When setting your goals, don't use general terms, like "increase sales" or "acquire affiliates." Instead, use specific terms such as, "Increase sales by 20 percent," or "Acquire five affiliates this quarter." Instead of saying, "Get more publicity," specify by saying, "Send out two news releases this month."

The big four.

Poker is one of my guilty pleasures. I play in small tournaments and occasionally in cash games. I often play at the same club with an older man who always seems to make it to the final table with a large stack of chips in front of him.

I jokingly asked him once, "When are you going to tell me your secret?" I certainly didn't expect the serious response I received.

"There are four keys to winning at poker—patience, wisdom, daring, and luck," he said. "Remember them, and you'll be in good shape," he added.

It occurred to me that those four elements also apply to winning in business.

Patience, as it applies to business, requires you to wait for your plan to come together. This does not apply to day-to-day business operations. When I am in, what I call, "full battle mode," waiting for even 20 minutes seems like hours. I want to get it done now. However, when it comes to implementing the entire business plan, I have learned to be patient.

Wisdom in business means having the information you need to make the wise decisions that help you achieve your goals. It also applies to the choices you make on a broad range of issues, including the vendors and employees you choose to work with.

Daring is another essential part of the winning equation. It means taking calculated risks, being bold and opportunistic, and seizing advantages whenever and wherever you can. Daring entrepreneurs break rules. They are not risk adverse. They scoff at traditional wisdom. If they feel that the time is right, they will often bet everything.

Luck is beyond our control. Or is it? I've always liked famed film producer Samuel Goldwyn's quote, "The harder I work, the luckier I get."

As luck would have it . . .

Don't minimize the importance of luck in determining life's course.

—ALEX TREBEK

Luck matters. In business, luck, having the breaks go your way, is so important that it's a shame we can't make our own.

Or can we?

Yes and no. In the literal sense we obviously can't. Lightning strikes simply happen. Some are carrying undreamed of opportunities for success, while others deliver totally unexpected news of cancelled contracts and payment defaults.

Most successful business people I know readily admit that luck played a big part in their success. "I was lucky to be in the right place at the right time," they say, or, "Opportunity happened to knock and I was smart enough to let it in."

But maybe it wasn't *pure* luck that put that person in that certain place at that precise moment. Maybe opportunity didn't just *happen* to knock on that particular door. Maybe those "lucky" people, perhaps subconsciously, were applying some rules or techniques that enabled them to get more than their fair share of the breaks every businessperson needs.

Psychologist Richard Wiseman, author of *The Luck Factor,* is one researcher who believes that you can make yourself a luckier person. "Lucky people generate their own good fortune via four basic principles," he says. "They are skilled at creating and noticing chance opportunities, make lucky decisions by listening to their intuition, create self-fulfilling prophesies and positive expectations, and adopt a resilient attitude that transforms bad luck into good."

In plain talk, what Wiseman is saying is this: Winners expect to win. They aren't afraid to play a hunch because they anticipate that luck will reward them. And they look at the bad luck that does, inevitably, come their way, as a bump in the road rather than the end of the world.

On the other side, we all know intelligent and capable people who seem to be followed by a black cloud. No matter how good they are at their trade, no matter how hard they struggle and work, they can't quite seem to escape bad luck.

Could it be that they have become addicted to bad luck? That their expectations that the breaks will always go someone else's way have become a self-fulfilling prophecy? Could the application of Wiseman's rules and a shift from negative to positive thinking change their luck?

There's a lot of evidence that it could.

I've always been an optimistic, positive person, and I've lived an extraordinarily lucky life. I could name a long list of wonderful and unexpected things I've received. I've had opportunities dumped in my lap and been blessed with the knack of often being in the right place at exactly the right time. Like anyone else, I've also had my share of disappointments, setbacks, and things that went terribly wrong. Still, over the long course of life's chase, I have been very lucky.

Recently I was experiencing some very bad luck. I was on a hard deadline to fulfill the requirements of a contract with a very large company. It was a contract with the potential for generating substantial cash for several years. When I was about half finished with the work, totally unforeseen events forced the person helping me to bow out of the project.

There was far too much work for me, working by myself, to complete before the deadline. The only thing that prevented me from calling it quits was my dread at having to call my contact at the company to tell him the deal wasn't going forward.

The next day, seemingly by coincidence, I met a person with precisely the right energy, skills, and enthusiasm to help me get the work done. I can't tell you how it happened. Maybe it was just a lucky alignment of the stars.

On the other hand, I can't escape the thought that my positive attitude about life and business had something to do with it. That my belief and expectancy that things will break my way was one of the hidden factors that caused me to delay making that dreaded phone call and give Lady Luck an extra day to smile on me.

Get a great assistant.

If the time arrives when you need an executive assistant, take your time and choose wisely.

Your choice of assistant reflects on you, and it will either make you look great or foolish. You need a trustworthy and experienced professional with first-rate communication skills. Pay him or her very well.

The best executive assistant I ever had was a mature woman. Her demeanor was both approachable and professional. She was all business, and her bearing commanded respect. In no time at all, she became a trusted confidante. She gave me her unwavering support, encouragement, and commonsense counsel. We had more than a hundred employees, and she often knew more about what was happening within the organization than I did.

Her advice, encouragement, and organizational skills were invaluable and deeply appreciated. When we sold the business and it was my last day on the job, I gave her a large personal check to show my appreciation. I did this even though I had made certain she would still be employed by the new management.

This is a position that requires a well-seasoned professional who wants to serve. Take your time to find the best.

Who says there's no free lunch?

To get speedy payment, our small software company offered a 2 percent discount if an invoice was paid within five days. A few companies took the offer, but we usually had to wait for most of the invoices to be paid in 30 days or more.

To get faster payment, we began including a small printed note with a headline that read, "Who says there's no such thing as a free lunch? If you pay this invoice within five days, you'll save [our bookkeeper would fill in the amount] and that will more than buy you lunch!" Far more companies began paying early.

A percentage is an abstraction—dollars buy lunch.

An offer you can't refuse.

Whether you are starting or running a business, the Service Corps of Retired Executives (SCORE) has an offer you can't refuse. These retired executives advise entrepreneurs on hundreds of business matters. Here's the good part: this confidential business counseling service is free.

Insights offered by SCORE executives are especially valuable in start-up situations. It's a good idea to have a volunteer look over your business plan before you launch.

These men and women know what they're talking about. They have spent years in the business trenches and can tell you when you are off track or on target. You can expect solid, no-punches-pulled advice. They can point you in the right direction.

Be a name-dropper.

Being a name-dropper in this context doesn't mean dropping the names of important people you know. It means dropping the names of well-known companies with whom you are doing business. "IBM, FedEx, and Xerox have all purchased our executive CDs," resonates with buyers and gives you instant credibility.

Find a hard-nosed advisor.

Find an expert who does not sugarcoat his or her opinions. This person should be someone, probably not a friend, who gives you expertise without regard to how painful you may find it.

I came to like hearing "You are way off base here, and this idea will go nowhere," because it is extremely valuable criticism. I want to know if I'm way off base. Since I don't want effusively positive feedback, I am cautious of enthusiastic agreement with my ideas. Unfortunately, friends and family have a natural tendency to give enthusiastic praise.

I once hired an experienced consultant who had worked for many years in the field in which I was starting my company. He described himself as a rogue entrepreneur, and he had started and grown several successful businesses.

While reading my business and marketing plan, he actually laughed aloud several times. When he finished reading, he handed my plan back to me and quietly said, "Good luck."

I asked him where I had gone astray. He didn't just give me his opinion, but he cited actual examples and case histories illustrating why some of the ideas were off base and had little or no chance of working. He suggested alternatives to the weak elements of the plan.

I accepted his advice, and I have no doubt that he saved me a lot of time and money. He gave me information that was tough to swallow, and I can't thank him enough for having done so.

Refresh your vision.

I often find that my vision can become clouded by being too close to my work. When this happens, I try to bring in "fresh eyes." Another set of eyes can spot (sometimes obvious) errors and omissions. An outsider can look dispassionately at your numbers and point out areas where you might be making mistakes.

Look for low-tech solutions.

You might not need those hours of programming on that expensive new software package to solve that sorting problem. Maybe you just need the people in the mail room to use a different-color label. In our high-tech business environment, we often overlook simple solutions.

Get two mentors: inside and out.

You should have two mentors. The insider will be invaluable for his industry-specific knowledge; the outsider will give you a fresh and detached perspective.

Work from home—or not.

If you're starting a business, you will want to consider working from home. Small start-ups and one-person ventures have access to a mind-boggling array of technological marketing tools. These tools were not available, or too expensive, just a few years ago. These new tools include powerful laptop computers, multifunction telephones, web-conferencing and e-mail marketing channels. Access to rapidly growing social media sites is a significant factor as well.

The primary drawbacks to working from home are the distractions you may encounter such as interruptions from family. You may also experience procrastination, induced by familiar surroundings. If these can be avoided, your new business has a good chance of growing.

Working on a business, whether from your home or office, requires focus and energy.

Unconventional wisdom.

Do not go where the path may lead, go instead where there is no path and leave a trail. — Ralph Waldo Emerson

"Think outside the box," is one of the most tired business clichés out there.

However, like many business clichés, it imparts some good advice.

The way things are done in business seem logical, and most companies adopt the usual processes without much thought.

If you have a consultancy, the best way to grow your company would be to treat your prospects respectfully and professionally. Right? Well, maybe not.

What consultant would tell potential new clients he's too busy to even talk with them or that their projects don't interest him? What consultant demands a 100 percent surcharge for rush work? What consultant generally treats potential clients as nuisances?

This style of doing business, while it seems like professional suicide, works for one web marketing guru who looked at the way everyone else was going after business and decided not to play the game. He wrote his own rules that clients had to agree to abide by before he would accept the work. He not only went against conventional wisdom, but he made a mockery of it.

I'm not advising you to take an approach this radical. I am suggesting that you experiment with counterintuitive ideas and find some that work for you.

From time to time, personally answer the company phones.

Spend an hour answering the phones now and then. You'll get a good idea of what kinds of calls your firm is receiving. You'll also gain an appreciation of how tough a job this is. (No, it's not beneath your dignity.)

Know your hourly burn rate.

How much does it cost to operate your business for a day? Divide this number by eight and post the answer in your office. You'll find that your tolerance for that 20-minute bull session in your sales department about Monday Night Football goes way down. Let this number guide you and your staff in how you spend your time. Another question to ask yourself is, "How much income must be generated per employee per hour to cover your burn rate and make a 20 percent profit?"

Don't be an incubator for future competitors.

It's an old and often repeated story: a top manager takes the three best salespeople along with a few other key people and starts his own competing operation. Have key managers sign noncompetitor/nondisclosure agreements when you hire them. Make it difficult for them to steal customer lists and records. Compensate them well.

Sharpen your negotiating skills.

It's not enough to enter a negotiation with just the idea of what you want. It is important that you have a plan. Your plan should identify any potential roadblocks to getting what you want. Once these roadblocks are identified, develop a plan to overcome them. This will include no-cost or low-cost offsets that you may offer the other party as well as a strong rationale for the other party to accept what you are proposing. There is a great deal of useful information available on negotiating.

The highest-paid profession is deal maker. When you look at the most successful people in the world, they achieve their success by being skilled negotiators.

You are competing against yourself and the clock.

Your only competition is you and the clock. You can't control the clock; it just keeps ticking. However, you do have mastery over how that time is used. Learn time management skills, and beat the clock. If you don't learn these skills, lack of time will be the biggest obstacle to your success.

Just bring it back.

My uncle sold his old Chevrolet to a young man. Although the bill of sale had "vehicle sold as is" in capital letters, my uncle got a call from the young man complaining about a problem with the car. I was surprised by how my uncle handled the complaint.

Instead of saying, "I told you the vehicle was sold as is," he said, "Just bring it back, and I'll give you your money back."

The young man continued to describe the problem, and my uncle told him again, "Just bring it back. I'll be happy to give you your money back," and added, "Other than that, there's nothing I can do for you."

My uncle was a keen student of human nature and knew that the best way to handle the complaint was to offer a full refund. When you look at the underlying psychology behind this, you'll see that my uncle established the value of his selling price by not hesitating to offer to take the car back. The move left the buyer with no place to go. He was either in or out. He was in. He said he wanted to keep the car, and my uncle never heard from him again.

Take a cab.

I had a mentor visit me when I was in the middle of a very harrowing business start-up. The economy had turned south. Company revenues had dropped. New customers were almost impossible to find. Bills were piling up.

He asked me the simple question, "How are you doing?" To which I replied, "I feel like I'm climbing a mountain and clinging to a sheer cliff."

He smiled and said, "I've been exactly where you are, but I discovered that there is a road to the top of the mountain, and you can take a taxi."

He instructed me to divert my attention from the problem and focus on a solution. He advised that I should take a couple of days off, get away from everything, and do nothing except think about a solution—that is, look for a taxi ride.

I did as he suggested, and the answer came to me. I went back to the same problem with a whole different outlook, renegotiated a few deals, bought time on some payables, and found cash within my existing customer base. I had found the taxi. I must hasten to add that it was a slow ride to the top, but I got there nonetheless.

Money talks to money.

A former business partner used to joke, "Any bank will be happy to lend you money if you can prove you don't need it."

I have found that few things are more daunting than trying to raise capital to start a business.

Forget banks as a source of capital. Pass on friends and family. Don't count on angels and venture capitalists.

This leaves you.

Start your business on a shoestring and build it to a point where it is bringing in sales. Then and only then go after investors. It's much easier to raise expansion capital than to raise start-up capital. If you have proven your business concept by creating even modest cash flow, investors will start paying attention.

Money loves speed.

Sales expert Nate Vitale first coined the phrase, "Money loves speed." I think this phrase could be restated as, "Money loves action," and the faster the action, the deeper the love. Those decisive thinkers who seize opportunities when they present themselves gain more than plodding decision makers. This basic advice is worth heeding.

Banish clutter.

In the early days of IBM, executives were instructed to have one sheet of paper on their desks at any given time. I have always assumed that this policy was to keep workers focused on one task at a time. However, it may also have been a way to curb clutter and promote uncluttered thinking.

Most of the successful business professionals I know are well-organized.

Clutter blurs focus. It represents the past and the unresolved. Time is lost looking for things. It drains energy.

I am not as organized as I should be. I let things accumulate and clutter my office, so I have a weekly office purge day when I throw out the unneeded papers and general accumulation of things I don't need.

I recently read that 90 percent of the time, once a document is put in a file folder, it is never seen again.

Get rid of anything that isn't useful, beautiful, or joyful.

Don't let work accumulate.

Before the advent of the Internet and online banking, I had a friend who would always go to his post office box with a small notebook containing his checkbook and a supply of postage-paid envelopes. He spent a few minutes paying his bills on the spot before leaving the post office. He never took bills home; they never accumulated. So instead of spending a few hours every Sunday afternoon over his bills, he was at the beach.

Small tasks that can be handled immediately should not be left to accumulate.

Get the right things done.

I've often heard people who are building businesses say that there are just not enough hours in the day, and they are right. Once you recognize this, you understand the importance of stepping back and focusing on what is important and prioritizing your tasks by asking yourself, "What is the best use of my time in growing this business?" There will always be fires to put out, unforeseen "emergencies," and minutia to distract you from moving the business forward.

The fact is that most of us take on far too much, and there simply is not enough time in the day to get it all done. Make the hard trade-offs for what is going to drive the most value, and put other projects on the back burner.

Banish the time bandits.

Work eight hours a day. That's it. The rest of the day is yours.

You can get a lot done in eight hours. In fact, eight hours is an eternity. If you don't believe this, fly coach for eight hours seated next to a crying infant. You'll get a keen understanding of just how long eight hours can be.

Consider the time you devote to productive work as your "Golden Eight"—golden because time is money.

Working a solid, focused eight hours is difficult. Every day time bandits knock on your door. Members of this mob include personal phone calls and texting, bull sessions with coworkers, checking personal e-mail, looking for lost things (highly productive people have clean and well-organized desks), personal errands, long breaks, and longer lunches. The list goes on.

It all adds up. Research shows that, on average, salespeople waste two hours a day. This works out to a startling three months a year! How much can you sell in three months?

By far the biggest time bandit is the Internet. While the web is indispensable for business, communication, education, and research, it is also highly addictive. Like most addictions, it devours your precious time, energy, and productivity and, by extension, your income.

Take it from a recovering Internet addict. If you are serious about increasing your productivity, avoid these Internet time bandits:

* *Social networking:* Sure it's fun to share photos and news with friends and family, but it also diminishes your productivity. Do it after hours.
* *Online videos:* That hilarious video of the cute kitten playing ping-pong is a must see, but not during the Golden Eight you've devoted to work.
* *News and blogs:* Offering lively writing, lots of photos, and tempting links to other sites and news items, these are powerfully addictive. Stay off them during work.
* *Shopping:* The Internet is open 24 hours a day. Shop before or after work hours.
* *Surfing the web:* There's a lot out there to see. It's interesting and entertaining but a pointless drain on your precious time.
* *All that other stuff:* Online games, auctions, adult sites, chat rooms, job sites, dating sites, and vacation and travel sites are all major workplace no-nos.

Each morning take a few moments to write down what you want to accomplish that day. This does not have to be an hour-by-hour work plan. It can simply state the work activities that give you the highest return on your time. Allow yourself a little flexibility, but follow your plan.

This will get you on your way to greater productivity. You'll enjoy the feeling of knowing that you've put in an honest and productive eight hours. You'll look forward with greater appreciation to the sixteen hours left for rest, relaxation, friends, family, and maybe a little time on the Internet.

I know one entrepreneur who actually has an alarm clock on his desk. After eight hours, the alarm clock goes off, and he goes home. While keeping an alarm clock on your desk may seem a bit extreme (and probably is not necessary for most people), it is a very strong reminder that you have eight hours to accomplish that day's goals, and as time ticks down, your production goes up as you increase your efforts to reach your goals.

Get off the phone!

Most calls should take no longer than five minutes. However, most people are so fascinated by the sound of their own voice that calls go on and on. Unless it's a sales call, get to the point and get off the phone.

Ask an expert.

When I need an answer to a particularly difficult question, I find that even the most renowned experts are surprisingly accessible. Whenever I contact experts, they give their advice and perhaps a few references for additional information.

They don't expect anything in return except my thanks.

Don't be shy in this area. You'd be surprised at the accessibility and generosity of experts in your field.

Stay out of emergency mode.

I have an attorney friend who left his phone at home and went on a two-week, twentieth anniversary cruise with his wife. When he returned, there was a stack of phone messages on his desk. Many were marked

"Urgent." He called the urgent ones first and learned that none of them was really urgent. In fact, many of the problems had been resolved.

As an entrepreneur, you will always have trivial urgencies and emergencies that can eat up time and drain your energy. Fortunately it's easy to recognize the difference between a real emergency and one that exists only in the mind of the person declaring it to be an emergency. Avoid dealing with manufactured emergencies. You don't become successful by sitting in your office overwhelmed with these. There's no money in your office. The money is out there in the world. It's your job to get your message resonating in that world.

Stay out of survival mode.

I have sometimes been consultant to companies that were in survival mode. Some I could help, while others were too far gone or didn't really want the help. Once in survival mode, the primary purpose of the company is shifted away from expansion and profits to dealing with creditors and making the next payroll.

Common reasons businesses go into survival mode are:

* Inadequate start-up capital
* Poor market research
* Disputes between partners
* Unqualified staff
* Weak leadership

As a consultant, I have sometimes noted a puzzling resistance from management to make the changes necessary to get out of survival mode. I have returned the retainer to these self-destructive types and wished them good luck.

Don't get caught up in office drama.

Office drama is not only annoying, but it distracts from work. Try to ignore it because drama decreases in proportion to your disinterest in it. Some people are addicted to drama, and if they can't find any, they create it to get a fix. If drama is being created continually and becomes a significant distraction, it is time to have a little talk with the offending parties.

8 GAINING ADVANTAGES

THE OVERARCHING GOAL of business is to gain competitive advantage and profitability through strategic planning and extensive market research. These elements provide the big-picture goal, but they are abstractions. There's a great deal of difference between designing a soaring cathedral and the skills and labor required to build one.

This chapter is not about "thinking big" but more about thinking small. It's about the parts, not the whole. In the business world it's all about the day-to-day operation, and every small advantage counts. Small advantages can accumulate quickly and dramatically improve your ability to compete.

If, at the end of a quarter, your revenues are higher than projected and your costs come in under budget, it will have more to do with your having gained small advantages than the initial big-picture planning and research. This is especially true in business where the marketplace is crammed with competitors who are fighting for a share of the money.

Understanding the importance of small advantages and having the skills to gain them are the keys to outfoxing the competition and growing your business.

Build something from nothing.

A woman from the Midwest found herself divorced, and her sole possessions were a van and less than $1,000. She was essentially homeless. She and her 18-year-old son hit the road. Instead of giving up, she took an action that has always been an inspiration to me. She found a supplier of an item purchased regularly by banks. She and her son, each with a roll of 50 dimes, began calling banks from side-by-side phone booths. Their pitch was simple: we'll deliver today and set you up on a regular schedule.

Many of the banks accepted her offer, and she soon had relationships with bank managers and other key personnel on her delivery route. If a bank manager was transferred, she followed him or her to the new location. Her business model expanded to other products for banks which she found she could supply.

She ended up building a multimillion-dollar business which was started from the back of a van.

And then there's the story of Rebecca the Muffin Lady. Her debts had piled up, and she desperately needed income. She was middle-aged and had no business experience or marketable skills. However, she did have a great talent for and love of baking. Her cakes and muffins were legendary with her family, friends, and neighbors.

Rebecca dressed herself as a pioneer woman. Her costume was complete with a sun bonnet. She began visiting high-rise office buildings with a large wicker basket filled with fresh muffins. In under an hour she would sell out.

Within a week she was carrying two wicker baskets. That still wasn't enough. She then began returning to her car to refill her baskets.

She quickly built up an enthusiastic following. Her arrival was an event announced by some companies on the intercom. Her debts were soon retired.

There's the story about a young man, just out of a drug rehabilitation program, who had the good sense to realize that to stay clean he had to sever all ties to his old life.

He left town in a beat-up truck with a lawn mower, edger, weed blower, shovel, and rake. His truck and tools plus the $800 in his pocket comprised his total net worth.

He relocated in a resort town far from his home turf. He started his business by driving around upscale neighborhoods looking for yards that needed work. He would make a list of the things that needed attention and approach the homeowner with a proposal to start work on the spot.

He did an excellent job and started picking up regular clients. Within six months he was fully booked and hired a helper. Within three years he had built the largest landscaping business in the area. He married and bought a lakefront home and raised a family.

He is proof that resolve and initiative trump adversity.

Put the hammer down.

Every successful business of any size has hammers. A hammer is a person, usually an officer or manager, who aggressively represents the company's interests.

Hammers are usually self-appointed. There is no special job title, and their roles are never officially acknowledged, but everyone knows who they are and what they do, which is, in the vernacular, put the hammer down.

Often, these people are quiet but extremely no-nonsense. They make it their business to know what's going on. Management will fire on their recommendation. Hammers represent the company's interests and keep work focused and on track.

Boys will be boys.

If you are a male negotiating with a male, avoid having a woman in attendance. From the schoolyard to the boardroom, boys like to appear strong to the girls. The younger and more attractive the woman, the tougher the opposition becomes. You are more likely to get what you want in negotiation if you are not fighting ingrained human nature fueled by ego and testosterone.

If the situation is reversed and two women are negotiating with a male in attendance, the same problematic situation could occur, but it is far less likely.

You need racehorses.

Your business will struggle if you are working with plodding people who want to collect a paycheck and nothing more.

Take your time to find and hire people who see your vision and are ready to work to help you achieve it.

The best employees have an entrepreneurial mindset and a winner's attitude. Interestingly, the challenge and the opportunity are often more important to the right people than the money. If you find such people, get them on your team.

Do not set up excessive requirements for reports.

The more time spent on reporting on what you're doing, the less time you have to do it. —MARK COHN, AMERICAN FOLK ROCK SINGER

Obviously you need regular sales and financial reports, but requiring people to set up new reports from other reported information takes people away from productive work.

Don't become a bureaucracy.

Bureaucracy defends the status quo long past the time when the quo has lost its status. — LAURENCE J. PETER, EDUCATOR

Be careful. As an enterprise grows, it tends to become increasingly bureaucratic and sometimes slowly loses the entrepreneurial spirit that fueled its growth. This happens when a small business mistakenly thinks it's a good idea to emulate the culture of a large organization.

Signs to watch for: a proliferation of forms, high risk aversion, resistance to change, departmentalization, sharply defined and adhered to policies, many memos, low employee turnover, centralized authority with a highly defined and rigid chain of command, excessive meetings and committees, personnel redundancy, stifled individuality and creativity, and slow growth.

Large organizations understandably develop corporate bureaucracies and procedures to avoid internal chaos. But if you don't fall into that category, avoid this trap.

Never allow a resignation to be withdrawn once it is tendered.

People tendering their resignation will not be with your organization for long in any event. Exceptions include a change in personal situations, such as, "Good news! I just found out that my husband is not being transferred, so I don't have to resign."

You had me at . . .

Whenever I'm recruiting for a marketing position, I always ask job applicants to send a résumé along with a letter explaining why they are perfect for this job. My reason for requesting the letter is to see how applicants promote themselves. If they can't market themselves, they probably can't market our products.

Many applicants send what I call a "feel good" letter. They write about being a team player, their multitasking skills, and their communication expertise. After reading a few of these cookie-cutter résumés, my eyes start to glaze over.

Occasionally, I receive a well-crafted letter in which the author gives a case history or two illustrating how he or she created marketing magic in the past. These letters often include specific numbers or percentages as in, "The plan I created increased revenues by 22 percent in six months." I give these applicants careful consideration.

A cover letter from one job candidate caught my attention instantly. It was just one sentence: "I can do this job standing on my head with one arm tied behind my back." I loved it! It was brash, funny, and immediately created a desire to read the attached résumé. The writer had accomplished his purpose.

I liked that the applicant had taken a calculated risk. Had the letter been received by a corporate recruiter, I doubt that the candidate's marketing skill would have been recognized. The recruiter may not have even read the résumé.

The résumé was strong, and I immediately set up an interview. Within a week, I hired him. He spent two years with the company and created and managed several high-impact marketing campaigns that increased sales and profits.

When I sold the business, he started his own marketing consultancy.

Who is making the reference?

Before you hire an employee or consultant, always closely check references and the people making them. Call them and keep them on the line. Get them talking. Learn more about their business. Ask penetrating questions. Then go online and check them out.

You'll be able to quickly learn whether the referring party is trustworthy and qualified to make a referral. More than once I have found that glowing references were coming from friends or relatives. Do your homework. Then hire.

Get sign-off on your policies.

Prepare a clear statement of policy and require that all new hires sign off on it, indicating that they understand and agree to abide by the policy. Important note: Your policies should cover only operations and employee behavior, rarely customer service or sales.

Run lean.

If you are always short an employee or two, then whenever that fantastic job applicant unexpectedly walks through your door, you'll be able to make a job offer on the spot.

Turn overtime into undertime.

If a project manager requests overtime, have the requesting party come in to do the work before the start of business rather than stay after hours. It's simply amazing how this policy cuts overtime expenses to the bone.

Learn how to be a public speaker.

The first time I had to address a group, I was terrified. I had notes, of course, and I had done some rehearsing. However, when I found myself standing before a live audience, I probably looked like a deer caught in the headlights. As I gave my talk, I couldn't help noticing blank stares and stifled yawns.

As I was leaving the podium, I made a promise to myself to learn the art of public speaking. I joined Toastmasters and learned what it really takes to deliver a good speech. Speaking is a lot like doing stand-up comedy. If you don't seize the audience's attention, your presentation will fall flat.

I suggest avoiding the pitfalls by opening with a humorous statement. It doesn't have to be a hilarious line, but it should be engaging and funny. Have complete mastery of the subject matter and project an air of authority. Avoid redundancy or you quickly lose your audience. Make your points, illustrate them, keep your presentation moving, and you'll leave the podium to the sound of applause.

You are who you think you are.

If you keep telling the same sad small story, you will keep living the same sad small life. —JEAN HOUSTON, AMERICAN AUTHOR

I once had a poor self-image. I didn't have a college education. I didn't have money or prospects. Back then, the concept of a self-image wasn't even familiar to me. It wasn't how people thought.

As luck would have it, I landed a job on a small ranch owned by a very wealthy man. He took a liking to me. Over the next year he showed me a different world. He and his wife sometimes invited me to their home for dinner.

He lent me books that we would later discuss.

Sometimes he would take me for a flight in his small private airplane.

Most important, he treated me with respect. My view of myself began to slowly change.

One day he asked me what my life plans were. I told him that I really didn't know. I explained that not having a college degree would limit my options. He looked at me as if I were crazy and said, "You are far more capable than 95 percent of people with degrees."

My self-image went up a notch again that day. I soon enrolled in night school, and my belief in myself continued to grow as I saw new possibilities for my life.

It wasn't until I was looking back, many years later, that I fully understood the profound influence his friendship and kindness had on my destiny. I realized what a powerful force self-image is and what an important role it plays in defining our lives.

Start looking at your potential. Redefine yourself, and you will change. You will start to see your true capabilities, and that knowledge will lead to a new you.

I'm sure my boss knew exactly what he was doing to help me. I have tried to pass his gift to me along to others.

Good guys finish first.

Unless we think of others and do something for them, we miss one of the greatest sources of happiness. —RAY LYMAN WILBUR, FORMER PRESIDENT OF STANFORD UNIVERSITY

I have had the honor of working with many renowned motivators and personal growth experts. While some have made millions, few of them are in it for the money. They all seem to have a genuine desire to help people. I have given a great deal of thought to what motivates them. They are primarily seeking happiness.

In some ways they have abandoned their egos and transcended the chase for wealth. They have a keen awareness of the fleeting nature of time and the impermanence of wealth and possessions. They become larger than life by giving to others.

Norman Vincent Peale said, "Somehow, the act of self-giving is a personal power-releasing factor."

If you are seeking true personal power and real wealth, lift others up and take them with you.

Build from the ground up.

Start by doing what's necessary, then do what's possible and suddenly you are doing the impossible. — SAINT FRANCIS OF ASSISI

Your first order of business in building a business is to test and deploy a sales and marketing strategy designed with one thing in mind—cash flow. Cash is more important than virtually everything else. It's the oxygen that's critical not only to growth but to survival itself. Without adequate cash your business sputters and eventually dies.

Many entrepreneurs focus on building their company's infrastructure instead of first building and installing the engine that ensures the steady flow of cash necessary for growth. This is exactly the wrong way to go about building a business. Cash flow is the life blood of business, so invest your resources in developing it.

You don't need all the money to build your business infrastructure up front. In fact, it is much better if you don't build the infrastructure right away.

Strong businesses are built incrementally. Think of building a business as ascending a flight of stairs. You wouldn't run and try to jump to the tenth step. Instead you would take them one at a time.

Build your company from the ground up. Avoid spending time and money building it from the top down, and always remember that there's nothing more important than creating and maintaining cash flow.

Develop a good elevator speech.

An elevator speech is a short and sweet summary that describes a product or service and its primary benefit. It's called an elevator speech because it delivers the summary in the time it takes for a short elevator ride, usually somewhere between 30 and 90 seconds.

A good elevator speech is a useful business tool.

Jill Konrath, founder of Selling to Big Businesses (STBB), explains why, "In today's fast-paced world, the average person is bombarded with thousands of marketing messages from multiple mediums every single day. Advertising is everywhere—television, radio, road signs, e-mail, banner ads, direct mail, clothing, pens, newspapers, and magazines. These pervasive and often intrusive methods of capturing attention have created a backlash; most people don't even notice them anymore."

The process of creating your elevator speech is a great way to get focused on what your company's central message should be. Having a concise, powerful statement that describes what you do and that reveals a benefit that is appealing to the self-interest of your listener will serve you well with prospective investors, employees, and vendors.

Things to remember:

* Shorter is better. I limit my elevator speech to 30 seconds.
* Do not use jargon or technical terms.

✳ Do not use business clichés such as, "We offer a 'best of breed' solution for . . ."

✳ The fewer the syllables and the shorter the words and sentences the better.

Your elevator speech should be delivered with enthusiasm. If you're not excited about what you're offering, why should the listener be?

Take the cash and let the credit go.

If a creditor offers a discount for early payment, take it. If not, negotiate one. This seemingly small item will add up quickly. However, make certain that the vendor doesn't give you the discount with one hand and then take it away with the other. To avoid this, negotiate the early payment discount after you reach agreement on the final price.

Clone Julie.

Julie was our highest-producing telemarketer. Not only did she have more sales, but her sales were 18 percent higher than the average. I sat down with her and asked if she would like to be "team leader" and receive a percentage of the increase in sales.

For the next week we recorded her sales calls. We picked 10 of her smoothest and most successful pitches and had each telemarketer listen to one each morning. After three weeks department sales were up by 7 percent, and average sales had risen by 9 percent.

Stop hiding from your buyers.

Telling you not to hide from your buyers may sound silly. What business would hide from its buyers? With the overuse of voice mail and the Internet, many organizations are doing just that.

"Your call is very important to us," but not important enough for them to actually answer the phone.

It started when some accountant figured out that if a business had a machine answer the phone, the company wouldn't have to pay a human being. The idea evolved and voice mail became increasingly complex. Why not, the accountants reasoned, "externalize costs" further by having callers spend their time screening and directing their own calls?

To protect the guilty, I'm offering a slightly fictionalized account of a call I recently made. All details except the names of the companies are real. I'm sure you've had similar experiences.

Brringg, brringg!

"Hello, you have reached Acme Industrial Wingnuts. For complete product, services, and company information, please visit our website at www.Acinwidgets.com. [*I am on this site. If I can get someone to answer a couple of questions, I am ready to order.*] Please listen carefully as our options have changed. If you know your party's extension, you may dial it at any time. For a company directory, please press 7. For customer service, please press 3. For sales, please press 4 . . ."

Great, I want sales, so I press 4.

Brringg, brringg!

"Hello, you have reached the sales department at Acme Industrial Wingnuts. No one is available to take your call. Your call is very important to us. Please leave your name and callback number, and someone will get back to you shortly."

I don't leave a message.

The next company I call actually answers the phone! A pleasant professional voice says, "American Allstar Wingnuts. How may I direct your call?"

I answer, "Sales, please."

"I'll connect you now."

A few seconds later I hear, "Sales, Mike Jones. How can I help you?" Mike, who was knowledgeable and articulate, answered my questions. My trust and confidence in the company soared. Mike then told me about a special they were offering. I liked it. He got my $7,800 order.

At some point sales transactions of any size require human contact. While the first company avoided the cost of answering the phone, the second got my business. I can't help but wonder whether the bean counters figured lost sales into the equation before celebrating the savings they realized by not answering the phone.

I am amazed at how many small companies put up roadblocks instead of creating a superhighway. I suspect that there are many folks out there like me who refuse to chase after a business so I can spend my money with it.

Are you hiding from your customers? Allow contact with the outside world, or else you are just a hermit trying to do business. Make it easy for everyone to connect with you.

Is the price right?

Avoid charging too much or too little. Test to find your right price. What you learn may surprise you.

You may be charging too much or too little for your product or service. With most, but certainly not all products and services, there is a great deal of elasticity in the price. I once consulted a firm that had a unique informational product it sold for $49. After testing (and against very strenuous opposition from middle management), I raised the price to $249. Unit sales actually increased!

Buy used furniture and equipment.

When I opened my first office, I made the mistake of buying expensive furniture and new equipment. Since I had no walk-in clients, I guess I was trying to impress myself. The thousands of dollars I spent on pricey furniture could have been put to far better use in building the business. Of course, this rule does not apply to any enterprise that sells goods or services to walk-in clientele where first impressions count.

Paper doesn't crash.

Always keep a hard copy. A hard copy is the ultimate back up. It's far easier to rekey 5,000 words you've already written than it is to try to rewrite them.

I have a friend who keeps a leather-bound notebook with him at all times. In it he enters random thoughts, reminders, things to do, and ideas. When I asked him why he simply didn't use his laptop, his response was, "Paper doesn't crash."

Success loves company.

Action is the foundational key to all success. — PABLO PICASSO

I have observed that success loves company in my own business life as well as in the business lives of others. With your first success, progress and growth become appreciably easier to attain.

You receive greater respect, and your opinions magically become important. You get easier access to money, talent, and publicity. People wanting in with you come knocking.

Everybody loves a winner. (But, as the song goes, when you lose, you lose alone.)

Barter smarter.

Bartering has been around since the dawn of human existence. It's a smart and easy way to get what you want by trading something you have.

Bartering is especially smart in today's economy. In fact, bartering has surged recently because it puts idle resources to work. Not only does bartering conserve cash, but it allows you to expand your business beyond your cash-paying customers. You'll find lots of willing trading partners out there who are more than ready to make a deal with you.

Bartering can be more than simply trading goods and services. Sometimes, both parties can get a lot more out of the deal, as this little story illustrates.

Against my friendly advice, my neighbor fulfilled a lifelong dream of owning his own restaurant when he bought a dinner house on the outskirts of town. Because it was run-down, he picked it up from the retiring owner at a bargain-basement price.

The restaurant needed extensive remodeling, including painting, carpeting, lighting, and paneling along with a lot of minor fixes. The restrooms needed to be brought up to code.

My neighbor got a bid from a large construction company that primarily did residential remodeling. Its bid to do the work was substantial.

A few days later, with the bid in hand, my neighbor went to the contractor's offices and met with the owner. He proposed that he pay 50 percent of the bid amount in cash and the balance in restaurant gift certificates. To sweeten the deal, he offered additional certificates amounting to 10 percent of the contractor's bid if the job was finished within 45 days of the start date.

According to my neighbor, the contractor laughed and said, "How the heck would we ever eat that much food?" My neighbor replied, "Use the certificates to land more jobs. Offer dinner for two with every bathroom or kitchen remodel."

The contractor, who did a lot of radio advertising, seemed intrigued with the idea. He said he would need to talk with his ad agency. Two days later, he called to say they had a deal.

My neighbor got a lot more from this deal than the restaurant facelift.

Shortly after the job was completed, the contractor began his advertising campaign. The contractor's hundreds of radio ads mentioned the restaurant by name! The dinner-for-two offer worked. The modest but steady stream of diners sent by the contractor, coupled with what amounted to free advertising, helped the restaurant quickly become a popular dining spot.

Ask and you shall receive.

I once consulted for a firm, and at the end of my engagement, the owner told me that the most valuable thing he learned from me was that everything is negotiable.

I always ask for a discount. I estimate that seven out of ten times I get one. I will ask, "What discounts are you offering?" to introduce the subject to the conversation.

Often, I am given one on the spot. If I'm not, I continue with, "I'm ready to buy now, but your price seems a little high. Can you do better?"

If the seller still doesn't offer a discount, I suggest a reasonable one. This offer is often accepted.

I am not embarrassed to ask for a discount when buying personal items. Depending on what I'm buying, I usually get a small price concession. While traveling recently, I stopped at a beachfront hotel to get a room for the night. I didn't have reservations. I explained to the manager that I wouldn't be using any of the facilities and just needed a room for the night. I told him that I didn't want to pay full price. His response surprised me, "How about 50 percent off?" I slept well that night.

When you have completed negotiations with a vendor and he or she has quoted figures, instead of asking, "What's your discount for early payment?" ask, "What's your cash price?" The word *cash* resonates with buyers because it describes something they're getting while a discount is something they're giving.

It's often more than the small percentage off the vendor normally offers.

No deal is infinitely better than a bad deal.

Don't get so caught up in the rush to close a deal that you make an unprofitable one. Always know your bottom line, and never go below it.

Information is money.

Having information before others do is literally money in the bank. During England's war with Napoleon, news was primarily delivered by horse and rider. If something went wrong with the delivery, there was no way to get the news.

The Rothschilds, however, received news of Napoleon's defeat at Waterloo via carrier pigeon. This allowed them to take big positions in the London stock market, knowing that when the news arrived by horseback, prices would soar. And they did. As a result of this use of information, the Rothschilds became one of the wealthiest families in the world.

While this is a dramatic example, it can be applied in any company.

Bootstrap your company.

I've done it, and I know that borrowing money to start a business is not a good idea. No matter how solid your plan, bankers and venture capitalists are remarkably uninterested in funding. You're a fledgling enterprise. Because of this, many entrepreneurs turn to friends and family for start-up money. This is bad business—very bad business. You are far better off starting small and slowly building cash flow. Once you acquire a solid "proof of concept," commercial lenders are all ears. By that time, however, you may not need them.

Negotiating is an inside job.

Large organizations usually have a complicated, layered, management hierarchy. You may find it difficult to finalize a negotiation in a reasonable time frame unless you have inside help. This means establishing a connection with a key negotiator within the organization. Once this person is sold on the value of what you are offering, he or she will become your champion.

Managers in large corporations look to advance their careers by completing profitable deals. When you have an insider, he or she will help you speed up the decision-making process better than you could do from the outside looking in.

Use this creative collection tip.

A friend of mine taught me this little trick. If you have a small amount owed to you and attempts to collect have gone nowhere, you may want to try this.

Get a filing form from the Small Claims Court. Fill it out completely, but don't file it. Mail it to the debtor with a handwritten note reading, "I didn't have the heart to file this without giving you one last opportunity to settle your account." Include a self-addressed postage-paid envelope. According to my friend, he receives payment by return mail about 60 percent of the time.

Try this and save yourself the time and annoyance of a Small Claims hearing.

Surround yourself with winners.

In my view, most people are on a headlong flight to mediocrity. They want jobs and may artfully and successfully get through an interview, but they are not really prepared or able to deliver excellent results.

I have sometimes hired people away from other companies when I was impressed by their knowledge, personality, and professionalism. I have turned sales pitches into job interviews. I once hired a liquor store clerk as a salesperson after visiting the store several times. He was intelligent and gregarious. After a few weeks of training, he was producing sales at a surprising rate.

In the early years of your company, make all the hiring decisions yourself because human nature dictates that managers never hire anyone more capable than themselves so the managers doing the hiring will be protecting themselves rather than hiring the best people.

9 | AVOIDING PITFALLS

Good things do not come easy. The road is lined with pitfalls. — DESI ARNAZ

THOUSANDS OF PEOPLE start their own business every day with little understanding of the hazardous road ahead.

The pitfalls are many. Some will delay you, and others will stop you in your tracks.

I've witnessed promising new enterprises that ultimately failed because precious time and money were wasted digging out of problems that could have been avoided.

Some hazards you encounter are mere bumps in the road. Others are nasty potholes. Some are landmines. Fortunately, many potential pitfalls are foreseeable and can easily be avoided. Others are more insidious, difficult to see, and can be triggered by the smallest of events.

No one is immune. You can have a red-hot product, a much needed service, or even a fantastic new invention and still never make it.

You will read about a lot of "don'ts," "avoids," and "nevers" in this chapter. You'll learn about some of the more common mistakes entrepreneurs make and how they can be avoided.

To ignore administrative pitfalls and legal traps in the road ahead is foolish. You'll go farther faster if you are running your business instead of working yourself out of quagmires that could have been avoided.

Beware the "expert."

The expansion of the Internet has given rise to a multitude of people who present themselves as experts. Many aren't, and doing business with them can be very costly.

No matter how slick their marketing or how cool their website is, I strongly suggest that you request a half-dozen referrals. Take the time to contact these referrals and ask questions about their experience with the company. Ask questions about price, delivery, and the quality of the work performed.

I once made the mistake of not doing my homework on a company offering expert website development. We discussed all the elements and functionality required for the website. I was assured that it was a "piece of cake" to get me everything I needed. I was told the job would take about three weeks.

After many phone calls and meetings which seemed pointless, it slowly dawned on me that I was not dealing with experts, but rather a company that held itself out as expert.

After eight weeks, I called the CEO and held his feet to the fire. He promised to complete the site within 10 days. It was completed; however, it took an additional three weeks, and the site never did function correctly. I had to spend more money troubleshooting and correcting the problems.

The company's initial low price was not a bargain, considering the lost time and what I had to do to get the site up and running.

I later learned that the delays were caused because the company was sending the work offshore, and it was having difficulty managing the relationship with the foreign company.

Avoid setting deadlines.

You need something no later than a certain date, but carving that date in stone does one of two things, and both of them are negative.

When you're working with others, you're better off not setting a precise deadline date, but tell all involved that the work is to be completed as soon as possible. If the deadline is too far in the future, it creates a false sense of security. Deadlines that are too short create panic.

However, if the deadline is particularly short, give those you're working with the deadline date along with a plan outlining how the team will meet it. Instill a sense of urgency in everyone who works for you. Time is indeed money.

Avoid writing memos.

I have received more than my share of poorly written, long, and rambling memos. Such memos confuse more than clarify.

I recently worked with a large company that sent 10 or 12 e-mails a week. While memos are an important part of business communication, there is no need for overkill. When you consider the time it takes for employees to read a high volume of interoffice communications, you start realizing the impact on the bottom line.

If you must write a memo, keep it brief. Generally speaking, the longer the memo, the more confused or frightened the writer.

Exceptions to this rule include technical updates, price change notifications, and other essential intercompany communications that require a written record.

Don't hire friends or relatives.

Top talent will probably not come from your circle of friends or family. While there certainly could be an exception to this rule, it's still a hazardous thing to do.

How do you tell the guy who was the best man at your wedding that he's fired?

Avoid importing corporate cultural viruses.

Much like a computer virus can slow down your computer, what I call corporate cultural viruses can slow down your operation.

If you hire someone who received experience at a large bureaucratic organization, there's a good chance he or she will import bureaucratic viruses into your organization.

I once hired an accountant who had been a department head at a regional gas and electric company. We hired him to put our accounting house in order, look for cost savings, and streamline our accounting system.

On his first day on the job he sent a memo to the entire staff instructing staff members in how to complete and submit a requisition request. It was long and detailed. I told him that there were only two people within our small organization who ever needed to make a purchase and even those requests were infrequent. I explained that they simply called me to discuss the need and get my authorization. He rolled his eyes and said, "You really should have a better system in place."

A few weeks later, I discovered from a manager that the new accountant was rewriting a section of the company's employee handbook and changing our policies regarding personal time off and sick days. When I asked him why he was doing this, he told me that the policies were far too generous, costing us money and "not required by law."

He had apparently seen no need to discuss this with me beforehand or consider the impact of these changes on morale.

I fired him on the spot.

Beware of reverse delegation.

My early business philosophy was, "If you want it done right, do it yourself." The problem with this, I learned, is that you quickly run out of time to do everything yourself.

I have since subscribed to Dale Carnegie's philosophy, "The secret to success lies not in doing your own work, but in recognizing the right person to do it."

Ah, there's the secret—finding the right person to help. Effective delegation requires effective communication, and even when you have excellent communication it's difficult.

When you undertake to delegate, you will get a crash course in the bad side of human nature. Reverse delegation is one of the major roadblocks to saving you time and accelerating business growth. Reverse delegation is frustrating and time-consuming and comes in many flavors.

Some employees' style of reverse delegation is to dodge responsibility by asking questions. Lots of questions. They gain their objective when you finally think, "This person is unclear, and it's going to take too long to explain. I might as well do it myself."

Another employee may ask for your assistance, which will require you to be responsible for a large part of completing the job assigned.

When this happens and you know he or she is capable of doing the job without your help, recognize it as a form of reverse delegation.

Hundreds of business cards, collected at a recent trade show, are being keyed into a database. The sales manager knows this, and he also knows who within your organization is entering the data. Yet he is standing before you declaring, "We can be making a lot more sales if you will get us those trade show leads." He's giving you an assignment. What's going on here? Why would an otherwise capable person come to you to ask you to do what he or she could easily do? You might need a degree in psychology to figure this one out.

Another form of reverse delegation occurs when an employee doesn't follow the simplest instructions and completely botches the job. This is a way of telling you not to delegate jobs to him or her in the future.

Never delegate the handling of an emergency or hiring, firing, or disciplinary matters. And above all, never delegate a task that you would not do yourself.

Beware of energy-draining people.

While the melodramatic term "energy vampire" smacks of the occult and late-night movies, there really are people who suck positive energy from a room as soon as they enter it. You will become drained and exhausted if you are exposed for any length of time to the negative energy these people throw.

You have probably had the experience of encountering a person who drained your energy. There is no scientific research on this subject that I am familiar with, but there is a great deal of anecdotal evidence for its existence.

Some years back we employed a part-time independent contractor who started his work at our office mid-mornings. When he entered our small office, you could feel the energy draining. This was mentioned to me by several team members. One of my colleagues likened it to a plug being pulled on a fan.

The contractor seemed to be a normal person although he was unusually quiet and never smiled. I am sure that his negative effect on those around him was unintentional. However, his presence really did cause others to become exhausted and unfocused.

It would normally be easy to simply walk away from an energy-draining person, but in a small office setting it's not always possible. I handled the situation by arranging for him to work from home.

The high energy, creativity, and fun were no longer interrupted each morning.

Have an "attorney avoidance plan."

Avoid lawsuits beyond all things; they pervert your conscience, impair your health, and dissipate your property.

— JEAN DE LA BRUYERE,
FRENCH ESSAYIST

Please note that I am not an attorney. The following recommendations are based strictly on my personal experience and should not be considered legal advice.

When I advise people to avoid attorneys, I'm not talking about business attorneys who provide essential services such as writing and reviewing contracts, maintaining corporate records, and working with regulatory issues and copyright and trademark matters. These are attorneys you need.

While you need the business attorneys, do all that is possible to avoid litigation attorneys. I am painting litigation attorneys with a broad brush, and I am certain that there are some who adhere to the highest professional and ethical standards. However, based on the many horror stories told to me by clients, as well as my personal experiences, I know that all do not.

Litigation can quickly drain your time and money, derail your business, and end up costing far more than the amount at issue.

A litigation attorney's interests, in most cases, are exactly the opposite of yours. You want a speedy resolution of your problem, and the attorney wants to bill you, at a high hourly rate, for as long as possible. I once watched a softball game with one team made up of the staff of a large local law office. The team's T-shirts were emblazoned with "Born to Bill." Funny, I guess, unless it's you who are paying the bill.

Here is how their game is played: The client is required to pay a large up-front retainer. As the case progresses, the attorney is paid his or her hours billed from the retainer.

While the bill is itemized, the client has no way of verifying the hours the attorney is billing or, for that matter, the necessity of the work that was done. Litigation attorneys love gray areas and are experts at delaying and manufacturing complexities.

When the retainer is exhausted, the attorney will demand that it be replenished, and your not doing so will likely result in the attorney dropping you as a client. The attorney makes no representations regarding the outcome of the case, of course, but wants that cash coming in.

It's not uncommon to learn that your attorney is on friendly terms with the attorney representing the opposing side. They both understand how the game is played and how it profits both of them. If there is one attorney in a small town, he or she will drive a Volkswagen. If there are two, they will both drive a Mercedes. Both your attorney and the opposing party's attorney are after your money. It's that simple. The judge, an attorney in costume, usually grants extensions and stays. The clock ticks on.

Avoid playing their game.

One obvious litigation avoidance tactic is to have clear up-front agreements with everyone you do business with, especially your employees.

Have a business attorney review all contracts before they are signed. Ask questions and get explanations. I always insist on a binding arbitration clause in my legal agreements. Arbitration is far cheaper and much less stressful than taking a matter to court.

Try to settle the dispute before you hire an attorney. If it is not a matter of fraud or some other egregious issue where negotiating with the other party would be fruitless, try to settle things yourself before a suit is filed. I once took the other party in a dispute to lunch. I brought the documentation to support my claim. We had a respectful business conversation. We agreed on a settlement before coffee and dessert arrived.

If the time comes when you absolutely must hire an attorney, hire the very best. This means expensive. The most well-represented party in a lawsuit usually wins.

One of the smartest things you can do to avoid attorneys is to know with whom you are dealing. If you are contemplating doing business with unknown companies or individuals, the means to find out detailed information about them and their reputation is easy to access.

Working with companies and individuals whom you know and trust may very well keep you out of court.

Don't get involved in petty principle battles such as, "It's not the money; it's the principle."

Your time is valuable; don't waste it on minor matters. If, in fact, it's not the money, pay the darned thing and don't do business with the offending party again.

File this under common sense (but read it first).We live in a highly litigious society. No matter how cautious you are, there is always the possibility of legal liability. First and foremost obtain legal advice, especially in the early stages of your business. Don't rely on your own interpretation of leases, contracts, or the laws and regulations governing your particular industry.

Another very important step to take is to separate your personal assets from your business dealings. Many small businesses operate as sole proprietorships or two-person partnerships, and if individual assets are not protected, they are at risk should the business fail or a legal judgment is made against the business.

Of course, business liability insurance is a must. If someone is injured on your premises, in most cases you will be liable for damages.

An often-overlooked consideration is backing up your data and having world-class virus protection. Data are an extremely valuable asset. So valuable in fact that, according to the National Archives and Records Administration in Washington, 93% of companies that lose their data for 10 days or more file for bankruptcy within one year. If you lose or compromise your data, you may not be able to fulfill an obligation, and this may cause you to break the terms of a contractual agreement. Know the law.

Sure, it may sound obvious, but let me make it explicit: there are myriad federal, state, and local regulations you must be aware of. There are millions of laws on the books in the United States. The U.S. Congress publishes federal laws every six years; the publication is over 200,000 pages long. Add onto this state, county, and municipal laws and you start to see the size of the problem. Failure to obey any law can be expensive and can cost you your business. Ignorance of the law is never accepted as an excuse. I know of a company that was named in a class-action suit for sending 100 unsolicited faxes. The attorneys behind these suits are ruthless, and the company being sued ended up declaring bankruptcy.

Bottom line: Get a good attorney to help in the beginning to avoid the bad ones later on.

Always strictly define work to be done when hiring an attorney.

Treat attorneys like any other vendor. Get at least three bids. Get an estimate of costs and time. Try to lock them into a set fee payable upon completion of the work.

Litigation attorneys love big, up-front retainers which they can draw on at will. Don't give them one. When the bill arrives (assuming it is not a set-fee arrangement), hammer them on any unclear or excessive items.

The majority of new businesses fail.

The reason that the majority of new businesses fail can be traced to several factors. Essentially the people starting the new business don't have an entrepreneurial mindset and are unsuited for the endeavor. Many don't have the fundamentals of good marketing research. Some lack good basic advice from a professional outsider and are relying on the cheerleading of their friends and family to make their decisions. Others are woefully underfunded. Still others have a dream that does not comport with the realities of the marketplace. Some proceed with nothing but hope and, as political scientist Robert Papes has written, "Hope is not a strategy."

Know your risks.

A ship is safe in harbor, but that's not what ships are for.

—WILLIAM SHEDD, AMERICAN
THEOLOGIAN

"Whatever made me think that starting a business was a good idea?" It's a question I have repeatedly heard in one form or the other from friends, relatives, and clients.

The deck is stacked against start-ups.

Unfortunately, there is no way to eliminate risk from business. A mentor once told me, "If anyone finds a way of doing business without risk, I hope they'll allow me to invest."

Before you plunge into business, give some thought to the ever-present risk factor. Be a little afraid. Have a talk with yourself. Assess your tolerance for risk. If it's low or you can't afford a loss, you might be better off working for someone else until the time is right.

If your decision is to take the advice of Stewart Brand, founder of Whole Earth Catalog, to "Stay hungry. Stay foolish," then you need to go forward fully aware of the hazards and always look for ways to lessen your risks.

Time slips away.

Napoleon reportedly told his generals, "I'll give you anything you ask of me, except time."

Years flick by as you grow older. In business, especially with a start-up, time also seems to accelerate. It's important to recognize the value of time and to conserve it whenever possible.

Twenty minutes wasted per day adds up to more than two weeks per year in lost production. Once you understand this, your tolerance for that 20-minute bull session on the latest reality show plummets. You work for eight hours a day, as do the people that work for you. Set the example. Let them know that you expect a full eight hours of work.

Loose lips sink ships.

The time comes upon every public man when it is best for him to keep his lips closed. —ABRAHAM LINCOLN

During World War II, propaganda wall posters warned that, "Loose lips sink ships." The posters were part of a campaign to tell people, especially those in the services, not to indiscriminately talk about defense subjects that could be of value to the enemy. It is a good rule to remember in business. There's the story of the attorney and the client who were discussing their next courtroom move as they washed their hands in the men's room, not realizing that the opposing party was in one of the stalls. Uh oh.

I once had breakfast with a friend who owned an attorney service. His business handled everything from filing documents to legal research to process serving. As breakfast proceeded, two guys were seated in the booth next to ours. It was a wild coincidence that they began discussing the formation of an attorney service that would be in direct competition with my friend's. We smiled at each other as my friend took notes. The information he gathered from their conversation was their strategy for acquiring clients. It included lower pricing, and quicker pickup and turnaround on some of the filings. They went on about the key accounts they were going to target and even gave the start date of their business. They also discussed a direct mail campaign they would launch.

Armed with this information, my buddy took immediate preemptive action. He met with managers and principals of the law firms who were his clients. He sent gifts to the decision makers. Besides strengthening personal ties, he also announced lower pricing that would match what his competitors were going to offer.

The competing firm was launched as planned. Although it landed a few small accounts, it had almost no success in wooing away the larger ones. The company folded within 60 days.

Here's a word on second acts.

Because you succeeded once, doesn't mean you will succeed again.

After a successful entrepreneurial stint, many people may fall into the trap of thinking that they can replicate their success in an unrelated field. The fact that you've made a small fortune selling on the Internet in no way indicates that you will be successful running a restaurant or starting a night club. This is similar to assuming that having a great career in professional basketball will put you at the top of the leaderboard at the next PGA tournament. It may happen, but I kinda doubt it.

If you are contemplating entering a different field, understand that it is a different ballgame with different rules and requiring different talents.

Build it, and they won't come.

If you build a better mousetrap, you'd still better have a good marketing plan. My longtime mentor, John Jaffe, often said, "If your job is to give away one million twenty-dollar bills, each to a different person, you better have an excellent marketing plan."

Can we talk?

In business, good conversational skills that build relationships are money in the bank.

Many people think that downloading an endless stream of information makes for a good conversation. You have probably fallen prey to a self-absorbed speaker countless times. You smile, nod, and interject an occasional "really?" Soon you have completely tuned the person out and are looking for a way to gracefully withdraw. When you finally escape, the clueless speaker leaves thinking that the two of you had a great conversation.

Businesspeople can take a lesson from the sales trainers who instruct salespeople to talk 20 percent of the time and listen to their prospects 80 percent of the time. However, if you're engaged in a business conversation, I think a 50-50 split works.

Remember that people love to hear their own names. It instantly creates a bond. It makes a connection on a personal level. Saying the name of the person you're talking to as you converse goes a long way toward solidifying a new relationship. If your buyer's name is difficult to pronounce, get the correct pronunciation from the receptionist or assistant. Write it out phonetically, and say it aloud a few times before your meeting.

Caution: Do not overuse the person's name or you come off as patronizing or insincere.

Don't call without a reason.

If you are waiting to hear from someone to move forward with a business deal, do not call that person without a specific purpose.

Calls that begin with, "I'm calling to check in with you to see how it's going," or "We haven't talked in a while, and I thought I'd just give you a call," are perceived by the person for what they are—timid attempts to prod.

Such calls are amateurish and put you in a subordinate position— and subordinates are easily dismissed. For the same reason, never thank anyone for taking your call or open with, "You're a hard person to get hold of!"

If it's time to prod the other person, then prod. You are far better served by being straight to the point by gently asking, "How much more time are you going to need to review the agreement and get back to me?" If this question kills the deal, don't worry about it. It was never going anywhere in the first place.

Can't miss, can miss.

An acquaintance of mine came up with a seemingly wonderful idea. He wanted to put advertising on the packaging for loaves of bread. He approached the largest regional baker in the Midwest and offered to purchase ad space on the bread wrapper. He had acquired large amounts of full-color books on birds of North America.

Back then, the books had a retail value of $30. He acquired them in bulk for $3 each. He placed his ads, offering the book at below its cover price. When he compared getting his message out on bread loaves versus direct mail, it turned out that the cost of putting the ad on the bread package was a small fraction of what it would have cost to advertise via direct mail.

It seemed like a can't-miss idea. Five million loaves of bread later, he sold only 37 books.

What went wrong: Had he tested his concept, he would have found that prospective buyers had no way to order the book other than sending their check to the PO Box in the ad. Although he had an 800 number, it was answered only between 9 a.m. and 5 p.m. Mind you, this was pre-Internet, and prospects couldn't go online to order.

Don't tinker with success.

If it ain't broke, don't fix it. — BERT LANCE, AMERICAN
BUSINESSMAN

You must change with the times. However, delivering a quality product and a consistent marketing message over time can earn you a fortune.

If your market is snapping up your product or service, don't change any part of the winning formula. Instead of trying to tinker with the formula in an attempt to squeeze a few more dollars out of the market, stay on course and keep it rolling in. This is not the time to redesign the packaging, add a few features, or change the price. That time will come later when sales start declining or when you can't keep up with demand. You've already found out what works. Ride the wave, and take the cash.

I have known marketers who seem to have an irresistible urge to tinker with success. I can almost hear one of them say, "Hey, if it's working this well now, wait until I fine-tune it." Tell them hands off.

Common sense dictates that if it ain't broke, don't fix it!

Is the job for you?

If you are selling a tangible item, not controlled by government regulations, you probably don't care who buys it. It's a simple transaction—you get paid, and they take delivery.

But if you are providing a service or constructing a customized product, the game changes. Consider the size of the job and the time it will take to complete it. Then proceed with caution. It's a good idea to develop certain standards that your customer must meet.

Is the client established and financially strong? Are the job requirements and delivery expectations realistic? Has the client unduly hassled you on price and payment terms? Why is the client switching vendors? Whom will you be dealing with?

Even though the money may look good, you can end up losing time and missing other opportunities by accepting a job that isn't right for you. Don't be afraid to walk away.

Avoid emotional involvement.

Just because you like a project, perhaps came up with the idea, and invested money in it does not mean that it is worthwhile. View all projects in an analytical and dispassionate light. If the numbers are not there, move on.

Don't carve things in stone.

A small magazine publisher that once engaged me as a consultant had the opportunity to acquire a successful, competing magazine on an earn-out basis. This means that the seller is paid from future earnings of the magazine without the buyer paying any money up front.

When I told him about this opportunity, my client summarily turned the deal down. When I asked him why, he simply said, "It is not in my business plan."

The publication in question was immediately grabbed by a smaller competitor who, almost immediately, acquired more subscribers and a bigger slice of the advertising pie. Within 18 months it became the number one publication in the industry. My client's lack of flexibility cost him several million dollars by passing on this extremely rare opportunity.

Make sure your business plan has the flexibility to exploit unexpected opportunities.

Don't put this off.

Nothing is so fatiguing as the eternal hanging on of an uncompleted task.
— WILLIAM JAMES,
AMERICAN PSYCHOLOGIST

Everyone is guilty of procrastination. It is part of being human.

Because you occasionally put off doing things doesn't mean that you are lazy or uncaring. There may be excellent reasons to delay acting: the issue is not that important, you are too busy with more pressing matters, or you simply don't want to do it.

Addiction to drama may be another reason. I once worked with a small magazine owner who always made his deadline by a razor thin margin. He apparently was addicted to the excitement of being late. He liked putting the coffee pot on and pulling all-nighters to get his little magazine to the printer at the last possible minute.

Before you decide to procrastinate, examine the consequences. Procrastination can cause problems beyond the obvious one of delivering a product late. It can make you anxious and leave you feeling discouraged and overburdened.

If you have a problem with procrastination, there is help but there are no quick fixes. The reasons for chronic procrastination are complicated. If it's time to take action, call in a professional.

Don't burn a bridge, even if you own it.

The printing company screwed up royally. It was a direct-mail piece, and although we had provided new artwork, somehow the printing company reprinted a mailing piece that we had previously tested. It was a big flop and failed to produce the sales we anticipated. We barely broke even.

Because of the expense involved and the schedule delay the mistake caused, my first instinct was to dump the printing company. At the very least I was going to give someone there a piece of my mind.

I called the company president and without even saying hello, he said, "We'll do it over immediately, and there will be no charge." A slight pause followed and he went on to say, "We will also print and mail your next job at 50 percent off."

The printing company delivered on its promise, and less than 10 days later the direct-mail piece was on its way. The new mailing pulled well. We rolled out a huge follow-up mailing and saved tens of thousands of dollars on the printing and mailing services.

I was glad I didn't get the chance to deliver a polarizing rant.

Avoid dogfights.

I was a partner in a small publishing and software company that served a narrowly defined business niche. After a year in business, my partner and I found ourselves being relentlessly attacked by a larger competitor which, for reasons unknown to us at the time, had become keenly interested in smothering our small operation. Its hostility went far beyond simple competitive fervor. The company did everything except mention us by name in its thinly veiled trade magazine ads that advised readers to, "Beware of counterfeits."

My first reaction was to mount a counterattack. My partner, who was older, and in retrospect, a lot wiser than me said, "Let them have their fun." He explained that, in a way, their attack confirmed that we were on the right track. He saw it as a form of validation. He said it would be smarter not to, as he put it, "Get involved in a competitive dogfight."

He counseled that we concentrate our efforts and put our time, money, and limited personnel resources into growing the company and not get distracted by the larger competitor's attacks. I reluctantly agreed to follow his advice. Our company continued to grow and gain market share at a healthy pace.

About a year later we had an "ah ha" moment when we learned that the competing company had been sold. The reason behind its behavior became apparent. It wanted to clear the field of a smaller competitor to enhance its position in the market and increase the value of the company.

Competition is good.

I have been up against tough competition all my life. I wouldn't know how to get along without it. — WALT DISNEY

Competition is good "generally speaking."

The existence of competition indicates the existence of a viable market. The presence of big players, of course, means that a big market exists. Always keep in mind that different markets have very different dynamics.

While the existence of big competitors means that a strong market is out there, that in itself doesn't give you a green light. It would be unwise to open a hardware store a few blocks from a national discounter. But it might be a good idea to open a drive-through burger joint across the street from a big chain's store. In fact, one small regional fast-food chain became a large national operation by doing exactly that. Its expansion plan called for always locating its restaurants on the same intersection as a national chain's. The larger national chain had spent the money and done the work in determining growth patterns, traffic patterns, and the demographic composition of the area. The upstart company essentially got all of this information at no cost. Brilliant!

A small aggressive entrepreneurial company, by innovating and differentiating, can usually outhustle a slow-moving bureaucratic behemoth. By offering a better, albeit more expensive, product some regional microbreweries have grown into international companies despite going up against gigantic and long-established competitors.

If you're in a small niche with lots of competitors that are all going after their slice of the small pie, competition is not a good thing.

If you are squaring off against a competitor the same size as your company, you will be forced to remain focused and work harder and smarter. Head-to-head competition is generally good for both companies.

10 SURVIVING THE HUNT

"HE WORKED HIMSELF to death" is not a figurative expression. It really does happen. In fact it happens more than you might imagine. The death certificates invariably say the victim died of "natural causes," which is usually wrong, since there is absolutely nothing natural about working yourself to death.

Business can be full of hassles, deadlines, frustrations, and demands, which all cause stress. There is a direct link between stress and a laundry list of diseases all of which can be fatal. Chronic stress can and does actually kill people.

This final chapter of survival advice may seem more fitting for a self-help book. What does this advice have to do with business? Nothing and everything.

My rules in the preceding chapters have been on the business of business. These are about the business of you.

Wellness is about your attitude and choices. A healthy lifestyle pays bottom-line dividends because it will greatly increase your effectiveness in business. Physical and mental well-being are not things you can buy at the corner drugstore. There are no pills or potions that will take the place of the everyday health-related choices you make.

This chapter is about more than just surviving the long and frequently arduous road we all must travel. It's about enjoying the journey. Here you'll find rules for keeping yourself in balance, stepping aside and releasing your stranglehold on your problems, gaining balance, laughing, smiling, and enjoying your life as you go forward toward your goals.

Dropping out is good for business.

Once a year you should drop out of business.

Disappear. Take a vacation far away from cell phones, computers, newspapers, radio, and television. These are electronic leashes that bind you to a complicated and stressful world. Simply leave them all at home. It's easier to do than you might think, and it will pay you big business dividends.

Get out of town. Get close to nature. Take walks. Enjoy sunsets. Sleep late. Read a good book. Nap. Laugh. Get some sun. Have a long soak. Go for a drive in the countryside with no destination in mind. Talk with the locals. Have a slice of pie. Smile. Breathe. Unwind.

Forget deadlines and obligations. Forget the clock. Eat only when you're hungry. Go to bed only when you're tired.

Don't stand in line. Steer clear of casinos, amusement parks, and big cities.

This experience will restore your spirit, enthusiasm, and energy. When you return to your work rejuvenated, you will have new energy, greater enthusiasm, clearer focus, higher creativity, and far better productivity.

At first, type A personalities (like myself) have difficulty understanding and accepting this advice. Anxiety levels rise just thinking about disconnecting. However, the business benefits, once understood, quickly dissolve any misgivings.

Reflect on this.

While the following reflections might seem more appropriate in a personal growth book than here, they have a very real bearing on both your business career and your life.

You are far greater than you imagine. You are a unique individual given the power to create your own life. When you understand and accept that you alone possess the power to define yourself and your life, dramatic changes begin to happen. You find new clarity, focus, and confidence. You also find that using this incredible gift is both exhilarating and challenging.

You are in charge. Think of your life as a movie. You are the writer, director, producer, and star. You choose your costars and the extras. Whether the movie is a smash or a flop, it is in your hands.

Your thoughts determine your outcomes. This is one of life's great mysteries. There are a lot of theories about this phenomenon, but no one really knows how it works. However, it does work and reveals the astonishing power of your thoughts. If you think you are average, you are. If you think you can't win, you won't. Conversely, if you see yourself succeeding, you will. If you expect great things to come to your life, they're on their way.

Winston Churchill said, "The price of greatness is responsibility." While I'm certain he was talking about fighting wars and leading nations, his statement applies to your life as well.

Life inevitably sends you your share of setbacks, problems, disappointments, and losses. These events are beyond your control. How you react to them is not. The choice is yours.

You have the greatness to persevere, to forgive, to smile, to lift yourself up, and to move on. Find your greatness.

Take a deep breath.

You've heard, "Take a deep breath," many times, especially when you are in a stressful situation. It's good advice that I would amend to, "Take a series of deep breaths."

When you are feeling frustrated, hemmed in, or stressed out, I recommend sitting quietly for at least five minutes and breathing deeply.

Deep breathing is an effective way to center yourself, clear your mind, and refocus your energy. It's a scientifically proven fact that breathing deeply for a few minutes causes almost instant relaxation in tense situations.

Fly with the eagles.

The body has its own laws. One of the most important is the law of circadian rhythm, which requires that you get adequate quality sleep on a set schedule. Get to bed early, sleep soundly, rise early, and you'll awake ready to take on the world. You'll gain a big edge, think more clearly, and be more productive.

Conversely, when you've partied until the wee hours, you won't accomplish much the following day. The folksy advice given to me years ago by my foreman at a steel fabricating plant says it all, "You can't wallow with the hogs at night and fly with the eagles in the morning."

Smile.

A smile is a light in the window of a face which shows that the heart is home.   —ANONYMOUS

Smiling and laughing boost your well-being, reduce anxiety and stress, and enable you to cope with difficult situations.

Weird as it sounds, you smile when you're happy and you're happy when you smile. The very act of smiling can make you happier, even if it's a fake smile!

Studies conducted by Robert B. Zajonc at Stanford University show that when you smile, facial changes have effects on certain brain activities associated with happiness.

Start smiling and laughing more today. Simply by acting like you're happy and enthusiastic makes you happy and enthusiastic.

Few things are more inviting than a smile. It invites a familiar approach and is disarming.

Sing out loud.

It sounds crazy, but it works. Just as a smile is powerful in changing your mood and releasing "happiness endorphins," so does singing. After a particularly stressful day, on my drive home, I crank up the tunes and sing out loud.

Keep it all in balance.

Bestselling author Robert Ringer has written extensively on synchronicity. Ringer's personal experiences led him to know the power of synchronicity. He points out that achieving life success is far easier if all elements of your life are synchronized. These elements include diet, exercise, work, and relationships. If all is not in sync, true success becomes difficult to attain.

Self-help author Brian Tracy puts it this way: "Just as your car runs more smoothly and requires less energy to go faster and farther when the wheels are in perfect alignment, you perform better when your thoughts, feelings, emotions, goals, and values are in balance."

I took a long weekend and compiled the following rules at a time when my life had become unbalanced and stressful. I was nearing a complete burnout. While I readily admit that I don't always follow all these guidelines, I do review them often, especially when the press of business and personal obligations is great. I find they help me regain focus and energy.

Your Outlook

Be generous with yourself and others.

Dream more.

Don't compare your life to others. You have no idea what
   their journey is all about.

Avoid negative thoughts of things you cannot control. Instead
   invest your energy in the positive present moment.

Don't overdo. Stay within your limits.

Your Relationships

Each day give something good to others.

Forgive everyone for everything.

Don't take yourself too seriously. No one else does.

Don't waste your precious energy on gossip.

Envy is a waste of time. You already have all you need.

Forget issues of the past. Life is too short to waste time
   hating anyone.

Make peace with your past so it won't spoil the present.

Don't remind others of their past mistakes.

No one is in charge of your happiness except you.

Learn a new word every day.

Smile and laugh more.

You don't have to win every argument.

Taking Care of You

Drink plenty of water.

Eat breakfast like a king, lunch like a prince, and dinner
 like a pauper.

Eat plenty of fruits and vegetables.

Play lots of games.

Read more books than you did last year.

Sit quietly for at least 10 minutes each day.

Breathe deeply.

Sleep for seven hours.

Take a 10- to 30-minute walk daily. And smile while
 you're walking.

Spend time with people over the age of 70 and under
 the age of 6.

Keep your sense of humor.

Try to make at least three people smile each day.

What other people think of you is none of your
 business.

Your job won't take care of you when you are sick.
 Your friends and family will. Stay in touch.

Your Life

The worst promise you can break is one made to
 yourself.

However good or bad a situation is, it will change.

When you awaken alive in the morning, be thankful.

Your innermost self is always happy. Follow it.

No matter how you feel, get up, dress up, and show up.

Separate fact from fantasy.

I wish that someone had told me early in my business career to separate fact from fiction. It would have saved me a lot of time and a good chunk of money.

Maintaining your optimism in business is crucial. However, if what you have worked on diligently for months is not making a profit, it may be time to take a cold hard look at your situation. It may be time to throw in the towel.

Quit? Never! You have been told many times to not give up. You are encouraged to get creative, to stay motivated, and to find a way to win. It's excellent advice up to a point. However, it is unrealistic advice if the time has come to cut your losses and move on.

When have you last taken a check? What are your credit card balances? How much money is in your savings account? What's your stress level? Are you happy?

Depending on your answers to these questions, it may be time to stop the wishful thinking and close your business. Take a detached realistic look at where you are headed. If you don't like the destination, it's time to change course.

If you decide to quit, put your ego aside and leave your comfort zone. Don't be embarrassed. Don't make it an emotional event. Don't beat yourself up. Know that you have made a smart business decision.

Just because you quit does not mean that you have quit for good. It doesn't mean that you can't find something new and start over.

Don't sacrifice your life on the altar of success.

I have found that being an entrepreneur often creates a stressful and unbalanced lifestyle. For the sake of your health and sanity, learn to detach yourself from your business. It took me a long time to understand this, and I paid the price.

I'd advise anyone, starting his or her own business, to work for defined periods of time, to vacation often, to pursue hobbies, and, most importantly, to spend time with friends and family.

Success without happiness is meaningless.

I met a friend who had moved out of our area and whom I hadn't seen for three or four years. I was shocked by his appearance. He was gaunt. A few minutes into the conversation, I asked him how things were going. He related that he had worked nonstop for the past three years on a business start-up. During that time, he'd not taken a vacation and had worked most weekends. His business had failed, and he lost a good deal of money. I can't help but think that his chances of success might have been greatly improved if he had taken vacations and time off whenever he felt tired. A lot of entrepreneurs burn out because of the high level of stress created by nothing as complicated as overwork.

See the end from the beginning.

The chase for success can lead to an obsessive, unbalanced, and unhealthy life. My best advice is to keep things in perspective.

Nothing else much matters if you don't have your health. C. S. Lewis wrote, "You don't have a soul. You are a soul. You have a body." To which I add, take good care of that body.

Rise above business. Wake up each morning grateful for what you have been given. Spend time with those you love.

Spend time with yourself, and do things that make you happy. Give your hand to others and help them find their way. Keep your integrity. Live a good life. Cherish your family.

When the hunt is over and you are sitting on your back porch on a warm summer night listening to the crickets, you will not say to yourself, "I wish I had spent more time on business and less time with the people who loved me."

That's all.

Directory of Rules

BECAUSE THE NAMES of the rules do not always comport with their content, we are providing a Directory of Rules and a place for notations for your convenience. Use this tool to annotate the rules that appeal to you and that may apply to your particular situation.

Index

About the Author

MICHAEL DALTON JOHNSON is an award-winning trade book and magazine publisher and a successful entrepreneur with over 30 years of business leadership. He is the founder of SalesDog.com, an educational and marketing website for sales professionals, marketers, and business owners. He is a highly savvy marketing professional and the creator of a product that has sold over 3 million units. He has appeared on NBC's *Today Show* as well as most major television network news shows. He has been a guest on more than 200 radio shows. Johnson has also been featured in leading publications, including *U.S. News and World Report, Time, The Economist, The Wall Street Journal, Los Angeles Times, The Washington Post,* and *The New York Times.*

He has a wildly diverse business background. Johnson is the founder of several successful businesses and the editor and publisher of *Top Dog Sales Secrets: 50 Top Experts Show You Proven Ways to Skyrocket Your Sales.* He currently owns and operates three commercial websites with offices in Carlsbad, California. In addition, he is the former publisher and editor of a national satire magazine.

During that time, he served as director of development for an international technical publishing and marketing company, which he took from three employees and two products to a multinational corporation with hundreds of employees and over 100 products.

At the age of 15, he dropped out of high school to take a full-time job. He joined the Army at age 17. After his service in the military, he worked as a ranch hand, factory worker, and construction laborer before venturing into the business world. He has never taken a business course and brings an unpretentious outsider's view to the subject of business.

The father of five, he and his wife Kathryn make their home in Rancho Santa Fe, California.